DEH313
Social Sciences/School of Education/Institute of Educational Technology:
An Interfaculty Third Level Course

# PRINCIPLES
## OF SOCIAL AND EDUCATIONAL
# RESEARCH

## BLOCK 5

### UNIT 22
**PRODUCING AND EVALUATING REPORTS**
*Ray Thomas*

### UNIT 23
**IN CONCLUSION**
*Roger Sapsford*

The Open
University

# DEH313 Course Team

Roger Sapsford, Senior Lecturer in Research Methods, Faculty of Social Sciences, and Course Team Chair

Michele Aylard, Course Secretary, Psychology

Andrew Bertie, Academic Computing Services

Judith Calder, Deputy Director, Institute of Educational Technology

Tim Clark, Research Fellow, School of Management

Jack Clegg, Producer, Audio-visual Services

Stephen Clift, Editor, Social Sciences

Sarah Crompton, Graphic Designer

Ruth Finnegan, Professor in Comparative Social Institutions, Faculty of Social Sciences

Adam Gawronski, Academic Computing Services

Martyn Hammersley, Reader in Educational and Social Research, School of Education

Fiona Harris, Editor, Social Sciences

Kevin McConway, Senior Lecturer in Statistics, Faculty of Mathematics

Ann Macfarlane, Secretary, School of Education

Sheila Peace, Lecturer, Department of Health and Social Welfare, Institute of Health, Welfare and Community Education

David Scott-Macnab, Editor, Social Sciences

Paul Smith, Media Librarian

Keith Stribley, Course Manager, Faculty of Social Sciences

Betty Swift, Lecturer in Research Methods, Institute of Educational Technology

Ray Thomas, Senior Lecturer in Applied Social Sciences, Faculty of Social Sciences

Pat Vasiliou, Discipline Secretary, Psychology

Steve Wilkinson, Producer, BBC

Michael Wilson, Senior Lecturer in Social Sciences, Faculty of Social Sciences

Consultant Authors

Pamela Abbott, Principal Lecturer in Sociology and Social Policy, Polytechnic South West

David Boulton, Lecturer, Faculty of Community Studies and Education, Manchester Polytechnic

Peter Foster, Senior Lecturer in Education, Crewe and Alsager College of Higher Education

Victor Jupp, Principal Lecturer in Sociology, Polytechnic of Newcastle upon Tyne

William Schofield, Lecturer, Department of Experimental Psychology, University of Cambridge

External Assessor

Robert Burgess, Professor of Sociology, University of Warwick

Advisory Panel

Peter Aggleton, Senior Lecturer in Policy and Management in Education, Goldsmiths' College, University of London

Jeanette James, Consultant Psychologist and Open University Tutor

Elizabeth Murphy, Research Fellow, University of Nottingham

The Open University
Walton Hall, Milton Keynes
MK7 6AA

First published 1993. Reprinted 1995

Edited, designed and typeset by the Open University.

Printed in the United Kingdom

ISBN 0 7492 0157 6

This text forms part of an Open University Third Level Course. If you would like a copy of *Studying with the Open University*, please write to the Central Enquiry Service, P.O. Box 200, The Open University, Walton Hall, Milton Keynes MK7 6YZ, United Kingdom. If you have not already enrolled on the course and would like to buy this or other Open University material, please write to Open University Educational Enterprises Ltd, 12 Cofferidge Close, Stony Stratford, Milton Keynes MK11 1BY, United Kingdom.

1.2

6403/deh313b5u22i1.2

# UNIT 22 PRODUCING AND EVALUATING REPORTS

Prepared for the Course Team by Ray Thomas

## CONTENTS

## ASSOCIATED STUDY MATERIALS

Three research papers from earlier in the course are set reading for this unit:

Reader, Chapter 7, 'Towards a methodology for feminist research', by Maria Mies: Section III and the Postscript (pp.73–82).

Offprints Booklet 2, 'Working with women's health groups: the community health movement', by Jean Orr.

Offprints Booklet 2, 'Health visitors' and social workers' perceptions of child care problems', by Robert Dingwall and Susan Fox.

# 1 INTRODUCTION: CRITERIA FOR EVALUATION

Many earlier components of this course have been concerned with the evaluation of research. This penultimate unit moves the focus of attention from the research itself to the ways in which the results of research are reported and presented. The aim of the unit is to describe the range and variety of factors that should be taken into account in evaluating a research report. The evaluation of reports is a common activity among academics and other researchers: the principle of peer review is well established. Research proposals and articles submitted to academic journals are passed to referees for evaluation. Reviewing books, which may report the results of research, is a responsibility of academics and researchers in the area. Examination of research reports is the standard way of evaluating programmes of research and the work of individual researchers.

Throughout the course we have looked at how research reports are evaluated in terms of the technical adequacy of the research they report, and this area of evaluation will be considered again in Unit 23. Here I want to look at a different facet of the evaluation process. Many of the criteria used for evaluation are related to matters of presentation and are similar to those of other writings — does the report, for example, give an adequate account of its subject matter: that is, the findings of the research? Is the report clearly written, coherent and consistent? Is the style of the report understandable and appropriate for the people who read it, and especially for the readers for whom it is intended? The evaluation of a research report is not limited to such apparently uncomplicated matters of presentation, however. It is not a simple matter, for example, to identify what might be meant by a phrase such as 'an adequate account of the findings of the research'. In focusing on presentation, account has to be taken of the nature of the contribution made by the research. Does the report exaggerate the contribution? Does it mistake the nature of the contribution, or understate it? In asking such questions about the contribution, account has also to be taken of other factors, such as the situation and motivation of the researchers or the broad aims of the research.

Evaluation can and should, therefore, take into account a wide range of factors. Some of these factors relate to the researchers themselves. What, for example, were their aims in conducting the research? The point of asking this question is that the nature of the aims can be used as a criterion for the evaluation of the research report. Does the report state the nature of the aims? Does it indicate the extent to which the aims of the researcher were achieved? The aims themselves can also be regarded as subjects for evaluation — were these aims 'appropriate'?

A second set of factors relates to the possibilities and constraints affecting the nature of the 'published' research report. What was the reason for producing the report? What is the nature of the intended, or target, audience? Is this the main report on the research, or is it one of a set of reports designed for particular audiences? To what extent has the nature of the report been shaped by its producers or editors and by requirements of an editorial nature? Were the researchers able to give a full account of their activities?

A third set of factors relates to the impact of the report. Did the report succeed with its target audience in the way the researchers intended? Did it influence the ideas of the target audience? Is the report likely to be influential on the way people think? Did it discuss the implications of the research for policy or practice? Has the report influenced, or is it likely to influence, policy or practice?

It is difficult to separate the evaluation of a research report from the evaluation of the research on which it is based. Consideration of factors of the kinds identified does not exclude the kind of evaluation criteria that have already been discussed at many points in this course. The ultimate criteria for evaluation of research relate to considerations such as whether the conclusions are true, whether they are supported by valid evidence, the extent to which the research is original, and the value of the new knowledge that the research has added. But the report does not usually contain all the evidence which may be required to evaluate the research on which it is based. In this unit I shall be looking at ways in which a research report, rather than the research itself, contributes new knowledge, and whether that new knowledge is of value.

The same criteria cannot be applied equally to every kind of research report: the purpose and function of the report have to be taken into account. The weight given to different criteria for evaluation of research reports varies with the factors relating to researchers' situations and the editorial possibilities and constraints. The next section of this unit aims to expand on these points by distinguishing five different types of 'research report' — theses or dissertations, articles published in academic journals, reports to the management of an organization, reports of stewardship and reports made in the 'public interest'. These types of report differ in the situation and motivation of the researcher(s) or producer(s), the nature of the target audience and the nature of what might loosely be termed 'editorial constraints'.

Section 3 and the later sections of the unit aim to discuss criteria used in evaluation and the weight that might be given to different criteria in the evaluation of different kinds of research report. I discuss criteria associated with assessing the originality of the report, matters of presentation and how a research report can be evaluated for consistency with other evidence. Section 4 discusses the factors which determine the influence of a report. Finally, Section 5 summarizes by looking at the range of factors that should be taken into account by making a kind of check-list that researchers, as well as evaluators of reports, could well have at their elbows.

## READING AND ACTIVITY I

Now read the following three research reports:

> Reader, Chapter 7, 'Towards a methodology for feminist research', by Maria Mies: Section III and the Postscript (pp.73–82);

> Offprints Booklet 2, 'Working with women's health groups: the community health movement', by Jean Orr; and

> Offprints Booklet 2, 'Health visitors' and social workers' perceptions of child care problems', by Robert Dingwall and Susan Fox.

As you read, think about the following questions:

- How would you describe the target audiences for these reports?

- How does this appear to have influenced the form of the reports?

Briefly make a note of your responses before consulting my answer at the end of the unit.

# 2 FORMS OF REPORTING

## 2.1 THE PhD THESIS

The PhD dissertation or thesis is sometimes put forward as the ideal form of report for the evaluation of research. Like all reports, it is distinguished from other research reports by the situation of the researcher, the nature of the content and the nature of the target audience, but the research is done by an individual, rather than by a group of people as is often the case with other kinds of research. The thesis covers work which has been carried out over a number of years, and a major part of the motivation in conducting the research is to obtain an academic qualification. The immediate target audience is two or more examiners who are expert in areas which are closely related to the subject matter of the thesis. The language used in the thesis may be that considered appropriate to specialists in the area, although these days examiners generally expect a clarity of exposition suitable for other academic readers who are *not* specialists in the area.

The rules for the content and presentation of a PhD thesis are individual to each university or teaching institution, but the general character of theses is standard. The thesis must include a review of the literature relevant to its subject matter. The content is expected to be original in a significant way and to demonstrate the competence of the researcher to conduct independent research, which usually means that the thesis must contain some collection of new material (of the kind which forms the focus of this course) as well as giving an analysis of the existing literature and other readily available information. The candidate, or student, must be able to defend the content of the thesis under examination by the expert examiners.

The candidate's principal concern is likely to be with the research itself and he or she may see the regulations on thesis content as requiring conformity to bureaucratic standards (e.g. in matters such as layout and the citing of references) and the acquisition of new skills relating to matters such as word processing and the reproduction of diagrams. The writing of the thesis itself may sometimes seem an unwelcome diversion from the conduct of the research, but the writing up should, in fact, be seen as an integral part of the whole process. Indeed, the PhD thesis gives more scope for the researcher to do justice to the presentation of the research results than any other form of publication. Thus the form of the thesis can be regarded as ideal for the presentation of research results for evaluation because it has been established *primarily* for the evaluation of the research and the researcher.

Phillips and Pugh (1987), writing under the title *How to Get a PhD*, identify four elements in the conceptual form of the PhD thesis — background theory, focal theory, data theory, and contribution:

1 A review of the literature is the standard way of demonstrating knowledge of the background theory. It is an attempt to identify the framework within which the research has been conducted. It defines the current state of knowledge in the subject area of the thesis. Typically, this review in a social research thesis would include reference to published statistics and other readily available data as well as studies relevant to the subject area.

2 By focal theory is meant an explanation and justification for focusing on the particular research which has been carried out. This element must identify clearly the nature of the subject matter of the thesis. It should, typically, describe and analyse the setting to identify the nature of the problem area, examine relevant arguments in the literature, articulate the hypotheses which may be tested, and indicate the use which is to be made of data to test the hypotheses.

3 The data theory component is concerned with the appropriateness and reliability of the data used. This component gives the justification for collecting the material on which the research is based, for using this and other material, and for the way in which it is used in the research.

4 The findings, or results, of the research are normally a central component of every research report, though Phillips and Pugh use the term 'contribution' to cover, not just the findings of the research, but also an explicit evaluation by the student of the *significance* of the findings. The contribution should discuss the significance, limitations and implications of the findings or results and so aim to identify the addition to the existing stock of knowledge which the research has made.

These four elements are seen by Phillips and Pugh as giving the conceptual form of the PhD thesis in all kinds of subject matter, not just the social sciences. This conceptual form is distinguished from the structural form. The nature of the structural form can be indicated by a set of chapter headings such as Introduction, Literature Survey, Methods, Results, Discussion, and Conclusions.

It should be noted that the presentation of research results is a relatively minor part of both the conceptual and structural forms of a PhD thesis. The thesis requires the candidate to explain, justify and evaluate, in full, the research work he or she has carried out over a number of years. The job of the examiners is, in effect, to validate the evaluation which the candidate should have already made in the thesis.

The proper evaluation of research, in other words, should consider a number of factors in addition to the results. The requirements of the PhD thesis as a form of report include the justification of the research, the quality of the material used, the limitations and implications of the research and, especially, the relationship of the results to the existing stock of knowledge. These requirements aim to provide a basis for the evaluation of the research and give the PhD thesis its distinctive character: other types of research report are not designed to provide as full a basis for evaluation of the research on which they are based.

Such requirements also determine the main characteristics of PhD theses. Theses are usually carefully argued and can be expected to score highly on coherence and consistency. They are complete and comprehensive and can include as appendices copies of documents which are crucial to the research — such as a copy of the questionnaire which has been used in a survey. They can also be expected to be well referenced, with clear indications of those ideas, points of evidence and arguments which belong to the author/candidate and those which belong to other authorities. The conclusions will be expected to demonstrate the 'contribution' of the research findings to the existing stock of knowledge and will therefore focus on developments in theory rather than on, for example, the social significance of the findings. Theses are generally written in a style which is intelligible only to an academic audience.

## ACTIVITY 2

Before you continue, make a brief note on whether you think the PhD thesis *is* the ideal form of research report for evaluation.

You will find my answer at the end of the unit.

## 2.2  ACADEMIC ARTICLES

A PhD thesis may be several hundred pages long, but the typical article in an academic journal may be only a few pages. Normally, articles will report on only part of the findings of a research project or survey; otherwise they have much in common with PhD theses. For example, articles in academic journals are expected to make a significant addition to knowledge in their field, and part of the motivation of the writer is usually academic advancement. Articles are also expected to be properly referenced — to list all the sources to which reference is made, in a form which makes it possible for others to locate them.

Articles submitted to prestigious journals which receive more submissions than they are able to publish are subject to a rigorous review-by-peers procedure. The author is expected to submit several copies, and the editor deletes the name of the author, and any other identifying information, from these and sends them for review to individuals who are regarded as being expert in the area of the subject matter of the article. The editor is then able to decide, partly on the basis of comments made by these referees, whether the article constitutes a significant addition to knowledge in the area and is therefore worthy of publication.

The target audience of such articles comprises academics. However, the sheer volume of academic publication means that the many articles written have comparatively few readers. UNESCO'S *World List of Social Science Periodicals* (UNESCO, 1991) includes 4,500 titles — starting with the *ASWEA Journal for Social Work*

*Education in Africa* (published in English and French in Addis Ababa) and ending with *Zimbabwean History* (published in Harare).

**Table 1   Serial publications in selected social science subjects in 1970**

| Subject | Number of serials |
|---|---|
| Social science general | 236 |
| Anthropology | 70 |
| Economics | 711 |
| Education | 286 |
| Geography | 118 |
| Law | 135 |
| Linguistics | 142 |
| Political science | 270 |
| Psychology | 177 |
| Social policy | 131 |
| Sociology | 101 |
| | |
| Total (of the above) | 2,377 |

*(Source: Line and Roberts, 1976, Table 3, pp.128–9. Based on data from Check List of Social Science Serials compiled at Bath University. The full check list also includes subject areas such as archaeology and architecture which are not usually closely related to the social sciences)*

This large volume of publication perhaps indicates that the primary function of many academic journals is as a repository of knowledge rather than as a general medium of communication — the value of publication to the individual author may sometimes lie in *acceptance* for publication rather than in a wide readership. Such factors mean that there is no requirement that articles in academic journals should be understandable to non-experts, and this in turn has led the requirement for an article to be a significant advance in knowledge to militate against readability.

The procedures to be followed for acceptance for publication are designed to ensure a level of quality, but it would be wrong to assume that the same criteria of quality would be accepted widely among social scientists from different backgrounds. The many different journals reflect differences in subject matter, ideology and approach to the social sciences — not merely differences in the area of application. For example, in terms of subject matter the Open University has a Faculty of Social *Sciences*, not a Faculty of Social *Science*. The social sciences represented at the University include sociology, economics, psychology, politics, geography and applied social sciences (including social policy and research methods). Each of these disciplines accounts for a number of journals, but not all the journals which can be considered as belonging to the social sciences fit easily into these subject headings. The classification given by Line and Roberts (1976) adds 'anthropology', 'education', 'law' and 'linguistics'. The UNESCO list gives a more detailed classification, including, for example: 'administrative science', 'business management', 'local government', 'management', 'personnel management' and 'public administration', most of which are likely to have been counted as part of 'political science' in Line and Roberts' classification. The UNESCO classification includes 'ethnography', 'ethnology', 'cultural anthropology', and 'social anthropology', as well as plain 'anthropology'. It does not include feminism, but it does include 'women' and 'women's studies'. The list identifies 'aging', 'criminology', 'family', 'social problems', 'social law', 'social welfare' and 'social work', as well as 'social policy'.

The procedures associated with the publication of articles in academic journals encourage a degree of conformity with the editorial policies of individual journals. The polite and proper response of an editor in rejecting a submitted article is to say that it is not considered as a significant advance in the field of knowledge covered by the journal, and to suggest that the article be submitted to another journal. For some authors, who meet constant rejection of this sort, the extreme solution is to establish a new journal whose stated approach and subject matter matches the kind of material they wish to see published. Although this is by no means an easy solution to the problem, it does occur from time to time.

The richness and variety of journals and their editorial policies have to be taken into account in the evaluation of articles. As I mentioned above, articles in academic journals are not addressed to a wide readership but to tightly, if not narrowly, defined audiences, and the conditions of publication favour a focus on tightly, if not narrowly, defined purposes.

## 2.3  REPORTS TO MANAGEMENT

Research reports written for the management of an organization — such as reports by individuals or teams within the organization and those by outside consultants — differ in many ways from both theses and academic articles. The most important difference lies in their aims. Whereas the aim of academic reports is to contribute to the advancement of knowledge, the primary aim of a report to management, from the point of view of both researchers and management, is usually to solve some organizational problem.

The most obvious criteria for evaluation of these reports relate to such matters as whether the problem has been clearly and properly identified and whether the proposals made would bring about a satisfactory solution. For the outside reader a lack of detailed knowledge of the organization will make it difficult to know whether the problem has been properly identified and, therefore, whether the proposals made would indeed bring about the desired solution unless they have been implemented and results obtained. In this instance, an important criterion for evaluation of such a report would be whether the report had been both accepted and acted upon by management.

The nature of the aims of a report to management, and the criteria of acceptability, will, of course, have had an influence on the procedures and conduct followed by the researchers and on the contents of the research report. The researchers may well have followed rigorously the principles of social research described in earlier parts of this course, but they may also have been careful to involve managers, and others who might be affected by the implementation of the findings of their study, in order to foster commitment to the purposes of the research and to increase the likelihood that the results and recommendations would be acceptable to them.

The importance of this involvement can be illustrated by practices associated with the conduct of Operations Research, or OR as it is usually called, and the OR report can be considered as an archetype of the report to management. OR began with the application of mathematical and scientific techniques to military problems during the Second World War. Since then, OR has remained a flourishing activity concerned with organizational problems such as stock control, queuing problems, distribution activities, and so on. It must have been apparent early in the history of OR that solutions to problems in this area, which were elegant and powerful in technical terms, were often not accepted by the organization as a whole. In the practice of OR the tradition of involving management, and other parties whose activities would be affected, has become well established. Consultation occurs at many stages — one commentator summarized this neatly by saying: 'OR is client oriented not solution oriented' (Eden, 1989). When finalized, few OR reports contain many surprises, and implementation of the recommendations is usual.

The major criterion for evaluation of the report to management is pragmatic: the technical quality of the solution found counts for little compared with the influence of the research and whether the report was implemented. This criterion is arguably also crucial for the evaluation of research reports to management which are predominantly social in their subject matter.

The function of a report to management can also be expected to have an influence on the report's style and content. It is unlikely that acknowledgement of the sources of information used, or references to sources of ideas, would be considered as important as it is in an academic report. The report should, however, pay respect to all the 'political' problems involved — carefully omitting even internal 'publication' of information of a sensitive nature and giving emphasis to the role of individuals whose support may be crucial to successful implementation. A report to management may also contain coded messages which are difficult, if not impossible, for the outsider to interpret and are therefore correspondingly difficult to evaluate.

## 2.4   REPORTS OF STEWARDSHIP

A further distinctive category of report is a 'report of stewardship' — that is, a report on how an organization or project has been managed. An annual report of a company to its shareholders is one of the most common examples of a report of stewardship, and is required by law. It includes a balance sheet and profit and loss account, and, in the case of a limited company, such accounts have to be certified as a true record by independent audit. In terms of the systematic production of new information about human activities, the company annual account could well be regarded as a social research report, but is limited in its contribution to new knowledge. The content of the annual reports of companies on matters other than the financial accounts is usually meagre and selective. The text which accompanies the financial accounts aims to engender confidence in the management of the company and does not include information which might be of value to competing companies or which might be exploited by customers or suppliers.

The most important kind of report of stewardship in social research is that made to the sponsor of a research project. An organization supporting social science research, such as the Economic and Social Research Council (ESRC) or a charitable foundation like the Nuffield Trust, will require annual progress reports and an end-of-grant report. For a major research project an intermediate body, typically called an 'advisory group' or 'steering group', may be specially constituted to oversee the research. Such an advisory group would expect to receive and to consider reports on the progress of the research.

Reports on the stewardship of social research projects are not usually expected to include the full detail of the substantive findings of the research. The detailed findings should be included in other reports which would normally be intended for publication. Rather, the report to the sponsors would focus on *how* the findings have been published in other reports and the extent to which the goals of the original proposal had been achieved.

The report to the sponsors shares some characteristics with the annual report of a company in that it is designed to show that the sponsor's money has been or is being properly spent, and concerned to give confidence that the project is being properly managed. For these reasons it is, like the annual report of a company, selective in its content.

The evaluation of such formal reports of stewardship is not the concern of this unit, but reports of stewardship form part of many other research reports. Elements of research reports which are accounts of stewardship should be recognized and evaluation should take into account the factors which influence them.

## ACTIVITY 3

How can the sponsors of a research report be identified? Who were the sponsors of the research described in the three papers you read for Activity 1? Make a note of your response before you continue.

You will find my answer at the end of the unit.

## 2.5 'PUBLIC INTEREST' REPORTS

Theses, articles in academic journals, reports to management and reports of stewardship are all relatively easily identifiable categories. The same cannot be said, however, of the wide range of social reports whose one common feature is that in some sense or other the motivation for publication is the 'public interest'. A report may be published in the form of a book, as a printed research report, as an article in a newspaper or in a non-academic journal, or as a radio or television programme. The target audience may be the public in general, or it may be some 'specialist public' such as those with an interest, or responsibilities, in the topic area, or those members of the public with an interest in the activities of the organizations which have responsibility for policy or administration in the area covered by the subject of the research.

An important category of public interest research reports is made up of those produced by research institutes. In the UK these institutes include, for example, the National Institute of Economic and Social Research, the Policy Studies Institute, the Family Policy Studies Centre and the Tavistock Institute for Human Relations, together with a host of smaller bodies specializing in a particular area or approach. The sole purpose and function of such institutes is to produce research reports. The target audience usually comprises policy makers and those believed to have an influence on policy, including government ministers, leaders of political parties, and civil servants as the advisers of government, as well as those who are seen as 'opinion leaders', especially the readers of such newspapers as *The Times*, *The Guardian*, *The Independent* and *The Financial Times*, and magazines like *The Economist*.

A further category of public interest report comprises surveys and other studies produced by specialist survey organizations. The most prominent of these are the Office of Population Censuses and Surveys (which includes what was known for many years as the Government Social Survey — see Moss, 1991) and Social and Community Planning Research. There are also many survey research firms which undertake work for public bodies, the reports of which are published, as well as market survey work for industrial or other commercial clients, the reports of which may remain unpublished. Some of the regularly conducted surveys and studies produced by these organizations were described in Unit 13.

The reports of Royal Commissions and other Committees of Inquiry can also be regarded as public interest research reports. The major areas addressed by such reports may belong to government rather than to social research, but the work of these commissions and committees is commonly supported by investigations which aim to follow the scientific precepts which are the subject matter of this course. Reports on such research may be included in the main report of the commission or committee and/or published separately.

These three categories all relate to research conducted at a national or subnational level. One of the main functions of many *international* organizations, however, is to produce reports which relate to social problems and conditions worldwide. An important recent example is the United Nations Development Programme (UNDP) whose first report appeared in 1990. UNDP reports are predicated on the assumption that 'the basic objective of human development is to enlarge the range of people's choices to make development more democratic and participatory' (UNDP, 1991, p.1). The 1991 Report makes extensive use of the results of existing studies and it also uses existing statistics from various countries to produce *new* measures of levels of human development.

There is a wide range and variety of other reports which can be considered as 'research reports'. These include public 'presentations' such as newspaper reports and television programmes. Reporters giving first-hand accounts of events they have witnessed, or investigative journalists searching libraries and public record offices, and seeking interviews with actors and witnesses of vital events, are performing activities which are usually focused firmly on some currently newsworthy subject matter, though their methods are parallel to those prescribed for social research in earlier parts of this course.

The producers of some television programmes have access to more resources to support research than are usually available to academic researchers. Such productions employ large teams to make investigations which consequently are more wide ranging, and may be of higher quality, than those carried out by academic social scientists. In the case of politically sensitive subject matter, television programme makers may be able to check and double-check on the reliability of key evidence involving a scale of expenditure that is just not available to the academic researcher.

## ACTIVITY 4

Make a note of what you think are the advantages and disadvantages, from the point of view of the researcher, of publication of research in a television programme.

My response is at the end of the unit.

Public interest research reports share characteristics with each of the four types of research report distinguished in the preceding sections. Like theses and academic articles, public interest reports usually make some claim to originality — if they were not saying anything new there would be little point in publication — but the newness is usually contrasted with accepted ideas rather than with the existing stock of knowledge.

Many public interest reports share some of the distinctive characteristics of reports to management. These are often addressed to social *solutions* as well as to social *problems*. They commonly constitute, in other words, policy-oriented reports. Their *primary* aim may not be to reveal new information, but to say what ought to be, or what might be, done about a particular problem or situation. Such research commissioned by government departments, for example, is, in general, intended to meet the needs of those departments. Thus the general aim of research done for the former Department of Health and Social Security was: 'to provide information for Ministers on ways of improving the efficiency and effectiveness … [of the Department] by promoting improvements in organization, operation and administration' (quoted in Richardson *et al.*, 1990, p.59). In the same way, the reports of Royal Commissions and Committees of Inquiry are specifically addressed to government or to ministries as the 'managers' of the country, and government and senior civil servants are an important part of the target audience for many public interest reports. In many instances particular government departments, or managers of other public bodies or privately owned organizations with responsibilities in the area covered by the report, will be specifically targeted.

In addressing policy issues, public interest research reports, like reports to management, may give more emphasis to some aspects of the research results than to others in order to be more acceptable to the organizations which 'manage' the area under study — thus a bias towards certain policies or proposals may be built into the reports.

Many other public interest research reports are addressed to the public rather than to government. Where reports of research are given in television programmes, or other mass-media channels of communication, they are usually addressed to a mass audience. Such reports typically identify a problem and discuss alternative solutions which may involve action by affected individuals as much as developments in governmental policies. Many such reports can be considered as expressions of 'critical theory' as developed by Habermas and Touraine (Habermas, 1987; Touraine, 1971, 1983: for example, as discussed in Unit 1/2, Sections 3 and 5). Their aim might be characterized as supporting the emancipation of oppressed groups by enabling members of such groups to recognize their true interests. Hammersley (1990), for example, points out that feminist reports, which define their goal in terms of the emancipation of women, as well as many studies carried out in the Marxist tradition, conform to the critical theory model.

Public interest reports also share some of the characteristics of reports of steward-ship. They are often produced by organizations whose *function* is to produce such reports and who often will have received specific grants to conduct the research which is being reported. The reports are written by staff who are, typical-ly, professional researchers whose job and responsibility is to conduct and report on research. Usually the report of stewardship components of a public interest report add to the quality and interest of the report. It is usually instructive, for example, to examine carefully the terms of reference which are normally included in any government-sponsored report. Such terms of reference should indicate the scope of the study and the constraints which the terms of reference may have imposed upon the researchers.

As with public interest reports which address policy issues, however, it is not tact-ful for the steward to amplify findings that would be unpopular or unacceptable to the funding body. As a result, the report may tone down the 'unpopular' com-ponents of the research and favour those which are more acceptable. Indeed, it is probable that there is a degree of self-censorship in most public interest research reports, though this will generally remain unseen. That a sponsoring body might require a report with a favourable bias becomes more evident when such bodies occasionally attempt to suppress a research report which is already in the public domain.

The researcher's starting point may be the lack of acceptability of certain ideas or kinds of evidence and the findings may not be consistent with existing cultural norms. In writing about such findings, the researcher must find a way to describe what the research has revealed in a way that will both be comprehensible to those whose understanding and thinking is shaped by conformity to existing norms and at the same time will *challenge* those norms. This process is made more difficult by the fact that the new findings require new language, yet must be described in the language which belongs to the existing stock of knowledge.

## 2.6 SUMMARY

Most reports, by their form of publication as well as their content, give indications of their target audiences and their classification within the five types of report considered here in Section 2. It is also true, however, that almost every research report will have some components which belong to each of these five types.

Most reports will, for example, contain some sections which exhibit the self-reflec-tive nature which is expected to be a part of a PhD thesis. Many reports will aim to identify both the existing stock of knowledge, as is expected of academic reports, and the nature of the conventional wisdom and/or the assumptions underlying public policy, as is expected of public interest reports. Most reports, as already emphasized, will contain some parts which are effectively 'reports of stewardship' of the resources invested in the research. Most reports will also pay some respect to the established authorities in the area of study and to the desir-ability of gaining the goodwill of the principal subjects, or actors, in the field, and so will have some traces of the characteristics of reports to management.

If you can identify different components of these kinds, you can usually add to your appreciation and understanding of a research report. The appreciation and understanding you gain will in turn contribute to the quality of your evaluation.

# 3 ELEMENTS OF EVALUATION

## 3.1 WHAT'S NEW?

Any research report should have something new or original to say, and it might be expected that the extent of the originality would be one of the most important criteria used in evaluation. In principle, originality can be defined as an addition to the existing stock of knowledge or as a contrast with widely accepted ideas. In practice in the social sciences, however, it is not necessarily so easily defined as it is sometimes difficult to identify and delineate the existing stock of knowledge about human behaviour and the nature of accepted ideas.

In the natural sciences it seems relatively easy to define originality. Copernicus, for example, made a significant discovery of originality in theorizing that the earth was spherical in shape and moved around the sun, instead of the sun moving around the earth, as was previously believed. It is difficult for us to imagine ourselves in the intellectual climate of the sixteenth century, but to put forward ideas which were considered so revolutionary that Copernicus's book was placed on the Catholic Index of prohibited books, and to imagine at that time that the earth could be round (something which was not confirmed by direct observation until Yuri Gagarin circled the globe several centuries later), seems to be a highly original contribution.

Maynard Keynes was a social scientist of comparable stature. One of Keynes' main contributions was to identify the kind of role which government could effectively play in managing the economy, and the principal value of his theory was that it was contrary to the prevailing theories of the classical economists. It is arguable, therefore, that the value of Keynes' contribution was iconoclastic rather than original.

A further difficulty in defining the stock of knowledge or the nature of accepted ideas is that knowledge of human behaviour which is relevant to the social sciences belongs to many different disciplines, professional groups and other specialisms. The social sciences focus predominantly on theory, but a number of professions — statistics, management, law, social administration, and planning, for example — which are also concerned with, and include a body of knowledge about, human behaviour, are more concerned with practice and are not necessarily included in the 'social sciences'. Taken-for-granted knowledge shared by a group of professionals over a particular period may not be shared with later generations of members of the same profession — or with social scientists. Knowledge can become unfashionable and forgotten about and might even become 'lost' because it is no longer part of the accepted culture.

In the context of the PhD thesis, originality is commonly contrasted with making a synthesis. The survey of the literature in a PhD thesis is a work of synthesis, but the contribution as a whole is expected to be original in the sense that it says things which are not contained in the existing body of literature. This might be something new, like Galileo's heliocentric theory; or it might be negative in the sense that no evidence has been found to support an existing theory; or it might 'reframe' existing knowledge to yield a different understanding. In the context of the PhD, originality is interpreted in terms of a significant contribution to the stock of knowledge — though that contribution can subtract from what was *assumed* to be known as well as add to what *is* known.

The acceptance of a criterion for 'contribution to the existing stock of knowledge' does not mean, of course, that social scientists can be expected to agree about any individual application of that criterion. But there is general agreement that this criterion also applies to other academic research. Such a criterion would not usually be appropriate to the evaluation of a public interest research report. As I mentioned in Section 2.5, the contribution of public interest reports is not primarily to add to the stock of knowledge, but to inform in some way or other. A public interest research report addressed to government typically presents its findings as a contrast to the assumptions which appear to underlie public policy or legislation, or as a contrast to 'conventional wisdom'.

The assumptions underlying public policy or legislation can sometimes provide tangible yardsticks whereby the originality of the contribution of research can be assessed. An example would be the non-recognition, until 1991, in English law, of rape within marriage. With the benefit of hindsight, it may seem obvious that this lack of recognition of rape within marriage could be demonstrated by the application of the statutory definition of rape to incidents within marriage. Research of such incidents showed that rape within marriage was a common occurrence (see, for example, Painter, 1991). It is arguable that the research had made a signal contribution by showing that the assumptions contained in the existing law were unjustified.

'Conventional wisdom' (or accepted ideas), on the other hand, is not easy to define or measure. The public image, as indicated by media reports, is often used as an expression of conventional wisdom and it is difficult to disprove the importance of the influence of public image, or what is perceived as the conventional wisdom, in many areas. As one of the founders of American sociology put it: 'if people believe a thing to be true, it is true for them in its consequences' (Cooley, 1909). Even a lack of clear articulation of the public image, or of any measure of conventional wisdom, does not usually inhibit the use of such constructions as a foil for the presentation of research results. The findings of a public interest report which aims to inform an oppressed group of its true interest, for example, will be at odds with the dominant ideology, rather than merely with conventional wisdom. Evaluation of such reports can be made difficult without the support of an alternative ideology (such as Marxism or feminism) to offer a critical interpretation of the dominant ideology.

For reports to management, or those parts of any report which are of a report-to-management character, the question of originality seems unimportant. The job of the researcher is to apply relevant knowledge to a problem in order to find a solution. If that knowledge is a well-established part of the existing stock of knowledge, then finding a solution may well be made easier because the knowledge to be applied has in all likelihood already been 'accepted' and does not challenge any dominant way of thinking.

In the evaluation of research reports, then, it may be helpful to understand the term 'originality' in its everyday sense — that is, research findings that are 'original' offer something new to the cultural assumptions of the target audience.

## ACTIVITY 5

Stop for a moment and think about the following question:

What are the advantages and disadvantages of this definition of 'originality'?

Make a note of your response before consulting my answer at the end of the unit.

## 3.2   INTRINSIC EVALUATION CRITERIA

Some evaluation criteria are intrinsic to the report itself in the sense that they can be applied without reference to other materials. The most obvious of these criteria are clarity, coherence and consistency. A report should be clear, so that its content is easily understood. It should be coherent in the sense that readers should be able to understand its structure, so that they can examine those parts of the report that are of special interest and relate them to the report as a whole. And a report should be consistent in the sense that different parts of it should be compatible and that no one part should contradict another. In practice, however, the application of these criteria is not as straightforward as it may seem.

## Clarity and the target audience

Assessment of clarity has to take into account the nature of the target audience. Clarity in a PhD thesis under examination by two or three specialists in the subject area, for example, is very different from clarity in a television or radio programme being viewed or listened to by audiences numbered in millions. Thus the first question to ask about clarity in evaluating a research report should be whether the report succeeds in being clear to its *target* audience. The assessment of clarity also depends upon the nature of the contribution of the research. Does the report clearly describe the results of the research? And does it clearly relate these to the cultural assumptions of the target audience?

The length of report allowed by a thesis or a book enables all these criteria to be met, but this may be difficult to achieve in any other single form of publication. Typically, the results of social research are fragmented in different forms of publication, and such fragmentation may even be becoming more common. A report for the former Department of Health and Social Security, for example, recommends that researchers should focus their publications on training needs, and, where the material is suitable, publish 'in womens' magazines ... journals devoted to health issues ... [and] newsletters published by relevant voluntary organizations' (Richardson *et al.*, 1990, p.22). This report further recommends that: 'Researchers should be required to produce summaries of their findings ... [which should be] widely distributed both by the researchers and by the Department(s) where appropriate' (ibid.).

The Rowntree Foundation, which is a major source of funds for social research, identified limited forms of publication as a significant problem:

> The tablets brought down from the mountain by researchers were more often than not encoded in dark and bewildering language. With rare exceptions, the finding blushed unseen in the pages of learned journals or languished in academic books which slunk slowly out into the world, often several years after the expiry of the research's sell-by date.
>
> (Joseph Rowntree Foundation, 1992, p.1)

The Foundation now requires all its researchers to write draft *Findings* on completion of their project, which are then published by the Foundation. In addition, the Foundation publishes a quarterly magazine, *Search*, in which journalists are commissioned to write pieces based upon research funded by the Foundation.

Shorter and more popular (wide-reaching) reports are often so clear about the conclusions of research that they avoid confusing the audience with the details of how it was conducted. A television programme reporting on social research, for example, may depend for its quality on a scientifically conducted social survey, but viewers are not usually given evidence relevant to the quality of that survey. The details of the survey itself may be published quite separately, although some of the conclusions drawn from it may appear only in the television programme.

As I have already mentioned, such diversified publication of research results is common and does not contribute to easy evaluation of research reports. Editorial constraints also affect all kinds of research report except the thesis. Editorial policy can bias the presentation of results; limitations on space can curtail opportunity to present explanations and evidence. Factors of these kinds can cloud the clarity with which the results of the research might otherwise be presented.

## ACTIVITY 6

Spend a few minutes thinking about how the target audience of a research report can be identified and note down your response.

My answer is at the end of the unit.

## Coherence and consistency

Coherence, in this context, is taken to mean 'holding together' and in this sense it may be the most important single quality to look for in any research report. Coherence at a strategic level means having the 'classic' structure of many essays, speeches and books, as well as research reports: that is, an introduction; the main body of the text containing, for a report, the purpose and aims of the research, methods used and the findings; to be followed by a conclusion. Stoddart, making recommendations on the format of an ethnographic essay, or 'organizing a socio-logical tale' elaborates only slightly on that simple structure:

> ... the introduction specifies what you are going to tell and why you are going to tell it; the section on data describes how you came to know the tale you tell in the findings; by way of concluding remarks, you provide a retrospective summary of your tale. If you do the job required by each part, you will find yourself on the way to writing sociologically.

(Stoddart, 1991, p.244)

The process of achieving coherence, as indicated by the last sentence of this quotation, can be as helpful to the writer of a report as to the reader. The process should include looking at the research from several different perspectives and asking how the research will look to someone who has no experience of it and what clues the reader might want in order to understand what it is about. Asking these kinds of questions when drafting the introduction enables the researcher/writer to think about the nature of the target audience and their level of knowledge of the subject matter of the research. It should also give the researcher ideas on how best to present the research results to the target audience. In a similar way, it is helpful to the researcher in writing conclusions to try to articulate generalizations and identify specific findings that seem worthy of emphasis for the chosen target audience.

From the reader's point of view, coherence of structure is important because it enables them to find their way around a report. It is similarly essential for the editors of newspapers, newsletters or journals, who are a key part of the target audience and who are sent a copy of the report for review. In order to send the report to the most suitable reviewer, the editor needs to be able to make a quick and accurate assessment of the nature its content and contribution: a clear structure makes such an assessment relatively easy.

Coherence at a more detailed level is mainly a matter of achieving consistency. It goes almost without saying that a report should be reasonably consistent in matters such as style and the use of key words: having a clearly defined target audience in mind can help achieve such consistency. Because the social sciences share so many words with the language of everyday speech, it can sometimes be good practice to include a glossary of key terms to clarify the sense in which the terms are used in the report.

Consistency also involves wider issues. Consistency between the conclusions of a report and the results of the research presented, for example, is surprisingly difficult to achieve. The conclusions often depend upon the relative weight given to different kinds of evidence, and the results of the research reported are usually only part of that evidence. The authors of a research report may believe that they have become experts in the field of study, and it is likely that this is how others will see them. As experts they are expected to come to conclusions. However, these conclusions may be dependent upon impressions, subjective judgements and other information that has not been systematically collected, and thus may not be wholly supported by the evidence that the authors were able to present in their report.

Sometimes a report can be *too* consistent — to the point where the conclusion that has been drawn would have been drawn *whatever* the results of the research. Students who have studied the Open University's social sciences foundation course, *D103 Society and Social Science*, may remember reference to a study of the consumption of food within the household relative to the 'social status' of the food. The 'social status' of the food was established by investigation of perceptions of the women in the households studied — not by any external indicator such as cost or nutritional value. One of the study's findings was that men consumed more 'high status' food than did women and one of the main conclusions was that 'the consumption of food conveys messages about the status of those that consume it' (Charles and Kerr, 1990). That conclusion is consistent with the report itself and the research results, but it is not clear that it adds much to the stock of knowledge. You may well ask: *what* messages does it convey? Bearing in mind that in this particular study it was the women who prepared the food eaten by the men, you might go on to ask: did the men in the study consume more 'high status' foods because the women awarded high status to the food they gave to the men, or because they awarded high status to the men themselves? Is the conclusion just a statement about the use of the term 'status'? What *is* 'high status' food? Would it not have been safe to come to such a conclusion without doing any formal research, beyond that required to show the existence of variation in patterns of consumption of food?

This particular example may seem trivial, but the kind of over-consistency it illustrates is one of the major criticisms levelled against studies carried out within the Marxist tradition and other 'ideological' positions. In the case of Marxism, for example, starting from premises about the nature of a capitalist society, many different kinds of social phenomena can be explained as the products of capitalism. Studies of this kind may be wholly convincing, but in evaluating them it is important to identify and separate new empirical content from insights which were already contained in the premises.

## 3.3    CONSISTENCY WITH OTHER EVIDENCE

Whatever the type of report, it can be assessed by comparison with other studies and by its consistency with other sources of information. The review of literature in a PhD thesis should include a discussion of other relevant studies and sources of information. Similarly, an article in an academic journal should at least make reference to other relevant studies and sources of information. As I mentioned earlier, in such academic studies there is a claim to originality and the making of that claim requires the inclusion of some kind of summary of the existing stock of knowledge in the area under discussion. This summary at least gives the reader a starting point for evaluation by enabling comparison with other sources.

Although an academic study will, typically, be well supported by other studies within its *own* tradition or set of paradigms, the value of many studies carried out within a particular tradition is open to question in terms of evidence obtained from research in *other* traditions and paradigms. Research based on experiments under controlled conditions, for example, may give results which are inconsistent with those obtained from observation of everyday social behaviour. Research based on observation of individuals and exploration of individual perceptions may give evidence which is quite different from that given by seemingly relevant 'official' statistics.

Such differences reflect a plurality of social *sciences* as distinct from any single unifying social *science*. The best research reports should bring together and deal with evidence from different social science approaches which can then be dealt with in a review of the literature and other relevant evidence. Reports which rely heavily on a single approach should acknowledge this limitation.

Public interest reports do not usually attempt to review the relevant academic literature, although they would be expected to quote relevant published statistics. The evaluation of such reports in terms of consistency with academic studies and alternative interpretations of published statistics may well involve entering the world of public debate and practical politics — a worthy role for the social scientist and one which goes beyond the subject matter of this course.

# 4 FACTORS AFFECTING INFLUENCE

It is extraordinarily difficult to assess the influence of research. One reason for this is the slight importance of new research results relative to the existing stock of knowledge. New research typically represents only a small addition to the total stock of knowledge and is often relevant only to a small part of the interest of those with specialist knowledge of the field. New research usually affects only a small proportion of the issues which have to be taken into account by those concerned with policy making, and it is usually relevant only to a small part of the body of knowledge associated with professional or organizational practice in the area.

A further reason why it is difficult to assess the influence of research is that influence is often not acknowledged. Response to new ideas is often governed by feelings as much as by rational thought. Research results which are seen as a small addition to the stock of knowledge are assimilated easily, but the initial reaction to results which are seen as radically new is commonly scepticism, rejection, hostility, or even refusal to acknowledge their reality or existence. Reactions of this kind may give a quite false indication of the influence of the research — when the area of study is revisited a few years later it may well be found that the ideas which were rejected or ignored when they were first published have somehow become absorbed into the existing stock of knowledge. Such a process may be a normal part of progress in the natural sciences as well as in the social sciences. The importance of such processes is consistent with the theory of scientific revolutions, based primarily on the history of the natural sciences, as propounded by Thomas Kuhn (1970).

How then can the influence of research be assessed? Or, more relevant to the immediate purpose, what qualities in a research report are likely to determine its influence? There are at least three answers to the latter question. First, the acknowledged influence of a report can be associated, negatively, with the extent to which the report is seen as being radical. Second, the influence can be associated with its authorship and sponsorship. Third, the influence can be associated with the degree and nature of involvement of those whom the report is designed to influence.

Whether a research report is seen as radical or revolutionary depends very much upon the style of presentation and, in particular, upon how the report represents the relationship of the results to the existing stock of knowledge. Research results can be presented as radical by giving emphasis to their newness and originality, or they can be presented as a minor extension to, or qualification of, the existing stock of knowledge by giving emphasis to the size of the existing stock of knowledge. The more emphasis that is given to their originality, the more likely it is that the report will initially be seen as radical and unacceptable. However, as noted above, such an initial reaction may not endure — the influence of the report over a longer period may be quite different. What was initially labelled as radical can come to be labelled as part of the established body of knowledge without any indication of how the transformation took place.

The meaning of 'authorship' is assumed to cover widely all individuals and organizations associated with the production of a research report. Two examples will illustrate the importance of this point in the context of assessing influence. If a research report which discussed birth control were to be produced bearing the imprimatur of the Pope, it would have a much larger impact on the millions of members of the Catholic Church than any number of reports on that subject which did not emanate from the Pope. A report produced by the Adam Smith Institute, which is regarded as a kind of think-tank for those who believe in the efficacy of market forces, will be received differently from an otherwise similar report produced by the Policy Studies Institute, which claims to be independent and to have a governing body including representatives of all the major political parties.

Research reports belong to one of three groups in terms of authorship/sponsorship. The most acceptable authorship/sponsorship is usually that which is part of the community for which the research is relevant. The least acceptable may be that which is seen to belong to a different, if not opposed, ideological tradition. In between are bodies which may be seen as independent. Such groupings may help to explain initial reactions to a research report, although, as we have seen, such initial reactions may not be a good indicator of the influence of the report over a longer period. The passage of time can transform originality and radical ideas, and research results which are initially regarded as 'foreign', into part of the established body of knowledge or culture of a community.

The degree of association of authorship/sponsorship with the community affected may be a much less important factor in determining the influence of a research report than the degree of involvement of the community with the research itself and with the process of production of the research report. I discussed the importance of this involvement in the context of the application of Operations Research in Section 2.3. Consultation with, and involvement of, the organizations and individuals affected, or of their representatives, can add to the acceptability of a report and increase its likely influence.

The involvement of the parties affected may be particularly crucial in the production of the research report. The circulation of a draft of the report to affected parties is desirable for nearly all kinds of research and such a stage can add immeasurably to the quality of the report by helping to make it more understandable to those who may be affected. Such a stage may also add substantially to the positive influence of the report. Some clues as to whether this stage has been carried out may be given in the acknowledgements which often appear at the beginning of a research report. The list of individuals and organizations given may include representatives of the main parties likely to be affected by the research, but the existence of such a list may be more useful in indicating that such consultations have been carried out than in indicating exactly who has been consulted. Some of the most useful comments on a particular draft report, for example, might come from government officials who prefer to remain anonymous in the final publication.

# 5  CONDUCTING RESEARCH AND WRITING RESEARCH REPORTS

Although this unit is primarily concerned with the evaluation of research reports, it may be useful to try and summarize by looking at research reports from a different angle. Instead of looking at the outcome, this concluding section examines the process of report production and the precepts the report writer should follow in order for the report to achieve its objectives.

As far as the *form* of the report is concerned, this unit has proposed two kinds of precept. Section 3.2 suggested that research reports should have the 'classic' structure used by many different kinds of writing, including reports: that is, a clearly identifiable introduction, main sections, and a conclusion. Section 2.1 suggested that a report such as a PhD thesis should have a conceptual structure with components dealing with background theory, focal theory, data theory, and contribution. All four of these components of the PhD thesis can be generalized to other kinds of reports.

The background theory in the case of an academic report, for instance, should summarize the existing body of knowledge relevant to the research. In the case of policy-oriented research, the background theory might summarize the conventional wisdom on the subject, or identify the assumptions underlying existing policy within the area of study. In the case of the report for management, there must be a summary of existing organizational practices as these relate to the subject of the research.

The report, whatever type it is, should deal with the focal theory component by including a definition of the 'problem' which has been investigated. In the case of an academic report the focal theory component should examine relevant arguments in the existing literature. A policy-oriented report should discuss the relevant assumptions which underlie policy, and it is recommended that a marketing research report should 'restate the background and objectives from the proposal' (Mohn and Land, 1989). The focal theory component might also include reference to some of the research results, or other evidence, which help define the nature of the problem which has been investigated. Again, whatever kind of report it is, it should deal with the data theory component by including a description of the methods adopted, together with an explanation or justification for the way in which the data have been collected and used.

A substantial part of most kinds of social research report is concerned with putting the research results into context. The time required to put these results into context, however, has implications for the planning of research. For example, it is not uncommon for research reports in the social sciences to be late in being produced, the most common reason for this being perhaps that the authors have planned only for the conduct of the research and have allowed insufficient time for relating the findings to the background theory. It is easy to underestimate the time needed for this latter stage — the existing body of literature typically has to be examined again in the light of the new findings, data from previous studies can seem to offer different kinds of evidence in the light of the new findings, and the new findings themselves are sometimes given new meanings when set against the detail of previous analysis and previously collected evidence. The yield of this stage may be rich in terms of the conclusions that might be drawn, but the iterative nature of the processes involved makes it more time-consuming than might at first have been imagined.

The time required to put research results into context in this way also has implications for the writing of research reports. It is rarely too early to start writing. Some writing about the context may have already been done as part of a research proposal; indeed, a summary draft dealing with the first three components mentioned above can be written before any data collection is started! The collection of new material will then require revision of this early draft, although many of the revisions will take the form of additions, and the nature of the changes required should help put the research results into perspective. In the word-processing era (which allows for easy amendment) such revisions have become much easier than they used to be.

A number of interrelated decisions have to be taken about the report. The *identification* of the target audience is crucial and will provide criteria and guidance for other aspects of the report — such as the length and style. Failure to identify a target audience correctly can lead to a lack of clarity and direction. The clarity and consistency which can be achieved if a report is addressed to a specific audience can also contribute to its success with other audiences.

Once the main target audience has been identified, a further decision can be made about the most suitable form, or forms, of publication. It is unlikely that any single form of publication other than a book-length report would either give scope or do justice to any research project which is the outcome of several years of work, as in the PhD thesis. It is also unlikely that the best way of reaching the target audience is through a report of such length. Such considerations may favour some diversification in the form of publication. It may make sense, for example, to prepare a comprehensive report to be made available to those with an interest in the detail, and then to select other forms of publication, as appropriate, for reports designed specifically for different target audiences interested in different aspects of the research. The form of publication, and any conditions of acceptance imposed by the publisher, will dictate the length of the report and the amount of space which can be given to different components of the report and to different aspects of the research findings.

A further, and sometimes difficult, decision that has to be made relates to the degree of emphasis to be given to what is new in the research, on the one hand, and to the extent to which the research results have developed from existing theory, policy or practice, on the other. As discussed in Section 4, giving emphasis to what is new may engender resistance, but playing down the originality of the findings may also do injustice to the originality of the research. An important aid to getting the balance right would be circulation of a draft copy of the report to individuals who could be considered as representative in some way of the target audience. Their comments might also help communicability in many other ways.

## ACTIVITY 7

This section has offered a kind of check-list for the *writer* of a research report. As a final activity, and to make sure that you have understood what this unit has been about, now make a check-list for someone *evaluating* a research report.

You will find my suggestions at the end of the unit.

# ANSWERS TO ACTIVITIES

## ACTIVITY 1

It is not immediately clear beyond doubt who the target audience for each of the reports is, but this is what occurred to me:

- The Dingwall and Fox paper follows the conventional form of a 'quantitative' research report — Introduction, Methods, Results, Conclusions, Discussion. As such, it is presumably aimed at an academic audience — at students and researchers in the areas of social policy and/or nursing. It was originally published in a collection of research papers aimed equally at nurses and nursing researchers, and it could clearly be of relevance to those who practise nursing or social work, or who organize the practice, or teach it. The presentation is relatively 'academic', however, and does not draw out conclusions for practice in any great detail.

- The paper by Jean Orr also follows this format, as much as is possible in qualitative research. (It is a report of just one set of incidents within a wider programme of research, and there are other reports covering different aspects of it in different ways.) Again, the original place of publication was a collection of research papers aimed at researchers and practitioners within an area of nursing (health visiting), who may be presumed to constitute its primary audience. It would also be of interest to a wider range of academics and researchers, and to those responsible for planning and implementing community health education. In my opinion, the easy and readable writing style makes it appropriate for all these audiences.

- The Maria Mies paper comes originally from a collection of essays on women's studies (Bowles and Duelli Klein, 1983), and the portion you read is part of a larger paper on feminist methodology. The target audience is, therefore, clearly, feminists and students of women's studies. This is not a formal research report, but a brief description of two studies to illustrate points made earlier in the essay; it talks about the form of the studies and their conclusions, but there is not much concrete detail about methods. The academic and philosophical tone of the accounts probably makes them more suitable for an academic audience — as it is, non-academics are unlikely to have been reading the book from which the article came.

## ACTIVITY 2

The PhD thesis can be considered a good form of research report for evaluation because it is, or should be, comprehensive in what it says about the research. But the typical thesis may be unintelligible to non-specialists and may make no attempt to discuss the implications of the research. It may therefore be the ideal form of report for the evaluation of *research*, but it is not necessarily an ideal form of research *report* for evaluation — except for evaluation by specialists in a specialized academic area.

## ACTIVITY 3

There is no requirement that a research report should include the information on who supported the research, but most research-funding bodies expect research reports funded by them to include an acknowledgement. There is no standard way of acknowledging support, but you will usually find that acknowledgement in the introduction or in a special note at the end of the printed report. If there is no acknowledgement of financial support it would usually be assumed that the research has been supported by the employer of the authors of the study, although such a supposition is not always justified.

Neither the Dingwall and Fox paper, nor the one by Orr, carries any indication of sponsorship or of there being a direct 'customer' for the research. Of the two projects described by Mies, one was organized and financed by its participants; the other was commissioned and funded by an international organization.

## ACTIVITY 4

The obvious advantage is in terms of impact. More people are likely to learn about the research than would by publication in almost any other form, and television programmes are often more memorable than other kinds of research reports. The disadvantages are that it is usually possible to publish only a small part of the findings in a television programme and that the impact may be ephemeral. A copy of the transcript may be made available, but access to the material published in a television programme is otherwise difficult.

## ACTIVITY 5

The advantage is that this definition of originality can be used for very different types of audience — academic, management, professional, public at large, and so on. The disadvantage is that it is a relative definition: it does not acknowledge any kind of 'true' originality.

## ACTIVITY 6

The most tangible indication is given by the form of publication. In the case of any serial publication, such as a journal or newspaper, or a regular broadcast, it can reasonably be assumed that a report is addressed to the readership of that publication. In the case of a book or other non-serial publication, it can be expected that the author(s) will identify the target audience in an introductory section.

These indications may not be consistent with the ways in which a report is written. Perhaps the most common single weakness in research reports is that the writing does not clearly identify the target audience.

## ACTIVITY 7

The ordering of such a list is an individual matter, but a check-list for evaluation should, at least, include the following questions:

1   Is the report coherent? Is it possible to identify the different components of the report easily?

2   Who is the target audience for the report? Is the style and language of the report appropriate to the target audience?

3   Are the findings expressed in ways which make them clear to the target audience?

4   Is the evidence that has been collected by the research and included in the report consistent with the findings?

5   Does the report explain and justify the methods used to obtain the evidence for the findings?

6   Is the status of the findings, in terms of newness or originality, clearly expressed in relation to previous studies, published statistics, existing policy, accepted ideas, and so on?

7   Does the report deal adequately with the question of consistency between the findings and any evidence from other studies and sources?

8   Does the report express the findings in ways which are likely to influence the target audience? Does the report indicate that representatives of the target audience were involved in the research and/or the production of the research report?

# REFERENCES

Bowles, G. and Duelli Klein, R. (eds) (1983) *Theories of Women's Studies*, London, Routledge and Kegan Paul.

Charles, N. and Kerr, M. (1990) 'Gender and age differences in family food consumption', in Anderson, J. and Ricci, M. (eds) *Society and Social Science*, Milton, Keynes, The Open University.

Cooley, C.H. (1909) *Social Organization*, New York, Charles Scribner's Sons.

Dingwall, R. and Fox, S. (1986) 'Health visitors' and social workers' perceptions of child-care problems', in While, A. (ed.) (1986) (reproduced in Offprints Booklet 2).

Eden, C. (1989) 'Operational research as negotiation', in Jackson, M.C., Keys, P. and Cropper, S.A. (eds) *Operational Research and the Social Sciences*, New York, Plenum Press.

Habermas, J. (1987) *Knowledge and Human Interests*, Cambridge, Polity Press.

Hammersley, M. (1990) *Reading Ethnographic Research*, London, Longman.

Hammersley, M. (ed.) (1993) *Social Research: Philosophy, Politics and Practice*, London, Sage (DEH313 Reader).

Joseph Rowntree Foundation (1992) *Review 1988–1991*, York, Joseph Rowntree Foundation.

Kuhn, T. (1970) *The Structure of Scientific Revolutions*, Chicago, IL, University of Chicago Press.

Line, M. and Roberts, S. (1976) 'The size, growth and composition of social science literature', *International Social Science Journal*, vol. XXVIII, no. 1, pp.122–59.

Mies, M. (1983) 'Towards a methodology for feminist research', in Hammersley, M. (ed.) (1993).

Mohn, N.C. and Land, T.H. (1989) 'A guide to quality marketing research proposals and reports', *Business*, vol. 39, no. 1, pp.38–40.

Moss, L. (1991) *The Government Social Survey: A History*, London, HMSO.

Orr, J. (1986) 'Working with women's health groups: the community health movement', in While, A. (ed.) (1986) (reproduced in Offprints Booklet 2).

Painter, K. (1991) *Wife Rape, Marriage and the Law; Survey Report*, University of Manchester, Faculty of Economic and Social Studies.

Phillips, E. and Pugh, D.S. (1987) *How to Get a PhD.*, Milton Keynes, Open University Press.

Richardson, A., Jackson, C. and Sykes, W. (1990) *Taking Research Seriously: Means of Improving and Assessing the Use and Dissemination of Research*, Department of Health, London, HMSO.

Stoddart, K. (1991) 'Writing sociologically: a note on teaching the construction of a qualitative report', *Teaching Sociology*, vol. 19, no. 2, pp.243–8.

Touraine, A. (1971) *The Post-Industrial Society*, London, Wildwood House.

Touraine, A. (1983) *Anti-Nuclear Protest*, Cambridge, Cambridge University Press.

UNDP (United Nations Development Programme) (1991) *1991 Human Development Report*, Oxford, Oxford University Press.

UNESCO (1991) *World List of Social Science Periodicals*, Paris, UNESCO.

While, A. (ed.) (1986) *Research in Preventive Community Nursing: Fifteen Studies in Health Visiting*, Chichester, Wiley.

# UNIT 23 IN CONCLUSION

Prepared for the Course Team by Roger Sapsford

## CONTENTS

## ASSOCIATED STUDY MATERIALS

There is no new reading associated with this unit but you will be referred back from time to time to various components of the course.

# 1 INTRODUCTION

In this final unit of the course I shall try to help you 'pull things together', to assess what you have learned and to help with the final examination. For the most part we shall be remembering, together, what has gone on in the earlier units, and I shall try to suggest units or associated readings that need to be re-read if any part of what follows is still obscure to you. (If you have no clear-cut answer to some of the questions which we shall be discussing, do not worry. Many of them have no clear-cut solutions, and if you remain puzzled then in some cases this will put you at the same level as the Course Team! If the problems are totally unfamiliar, however, you probably need to go back and re-read some of the text.) Within each section a revision guide will be provided, to act as an 'index' to the course and to help with your pre-examination work.

In what follows, Section 2 is concerned with the 'technical' side of research: what researchers have to do to provide acceptable evidence that their research conclusions are true. The other three sections are concerned with other aspects of the assessment of research. Section 3 looks at the relevance of research and asks the question 'Relevant for what?' This leads us on into a discussion of the 'external' aspects of research — the relationship of research to theory, to policy and to practice. Section 4 is more reflexive, looking at 'internal' aspects of research programmes and theories — the ways in which what we take for granted in our everyday lives is also taken for granted in research (often thereby supporting one side of a 'political' issue at the expense of another), and how we can perhaps start to overcome our own 'cultural blinkers'. The fifth section is on the ethics of research — the relationship of the researcher to the 'subjects' of the research and their interests and to the needs and interests of the wider society. (It might be argued that the topic areas of Sections 4 and 5 — underlying, as they do, all the decisions we make about research — should have come first in the unit. They are placed where they are because we need to understand the technicalities of research and its social context before we can fully consider the political and ethical impact of these.)

# 2 VALIDITY

We have assumed as basic in this course that the first goal of research is discovering truth about the world, because to assume anything else leads to an incoherent argument, as we saw in Block 1. We are well aware of the claims that have been made for the primacy of other goals. One may reasonably claim, for example, that research is of no use which is of no use — that a research report is to be judged by what it contributes to theory or policy or practice. We would entirely agree with these claims. However, a prior requirement of research conclusions is that they be *true*, or at least a credible approximation to the truth. What makes research useful for theory or policy or practice is that one may believe its conclusions (within the limitations and qualifications that may be appropriate to the particular study). If it were not able to make this claim, it would be of no use, however much it supported a position which we wished to adopt and support. The first requirement of research, therefore, is that it leads — in so far as it can — to true conclusions.

Truth which is discovered about the world (as opposed to the 'logical truth' to be deduced from definitions) is seldom self-evident. While some have argued for some kind of 'absolute' set of credentials against which truth can be measured, we have followed Martyn Hammersley in the first block of the course in rejecting this kind of position as ultimately untenable. That being so, the research report takes the form of an *argument*. We start with a question, or an area to be investigated, and finish with conclusions about it. In between comes the evidence on which these conclusions are based, and we *argue* that the conclusions are credible on the basis of this evidence.

## REVISION GUIDE

If you do not remember the arguments about the nature of truth in Block 1, you may wish to revise them now.

The arguments about the aims of research, and the secondary nature of utility as an aim of research, may be found in Unit 1/2, Sections 3, 5 and 7, and Unit 3/4, Section 2.1. See also Section 5 of Unit 16 and Section 2 of Unit 22.

The argument that there is no ultimate criterion or set of criteria against which we can measure truth is to be found in Unit 1/2, Section 3.2.

Within the broad argument which the research report constitutes there are many smaller arguments, about the quality of the evidence — its *validity*, the extent to which it can be taken as meaning what the researcher wishes to claim it means. The rest of this section looks at the types of argument about the validity of evidence, under the sub-headings of 'case selection', 'the suitability of comparisons' and 'data collection and measurement'. It is worth noting at this point, however, that validity is not an absolute quality, something which an argument possesses or does not possess. Rather, we assess the *degree* to which a part of the argument is valid, and therefore the extent to which the whole may be believed.

## 2.1  CASE SELECTION

One of the first questions we are likely to ask about a piece of research is whether the 'units of analysis' are appropriate to the problems being tackled and the conclusions being drawn. By 'units of analysis' I mean the 'objects' of the research — often people, but sometimes families, schools, hospitals, geographical areas (e.g. the Census wards which were the units of analysis in Abbott *et al.*, 1992), etc. Survey research often makes explicit claims to *represent* a population, and the technology of sampling is designed to back up these claims. Representation is clearly of the utmost importance if claims are being made about the proportion of a population who fall into some designated category. Where the research is concerned with the relationship of characteristics *within* individuals or other units of analysis, evidence that the sample is fully representative of its population may be less crucial, but the question still arises; it would be unwise, for example, to base generalizations about the human race on research which explored the characteristics of only one gender or class or age-group. Some kinds of research often make fewer explicit claims — particularly where one or a small number of cases is being explored in depth — but we will still be inclined to ask whether the cases are appropriate for the argument. Are they, for example, in some way *typical* of the population to which we wish to generalize; as, say, the nurse interviewed on the audio-cassette 'An unstructured interview' is treated as a 'typical nurse'? Or do they cover the range of kinds of cases, even if not in the proportions to be found in the population (as in the Abbott and Sapsford 1987 paper on mothers of mentally handicapped children which you read in Block 2)? Are they in some interesting way extreme, or 'crucial cases' — cases where some hypothesized pattern ought to be found if it is to be found anywhere at all? Whatever the nature of the research, a research paper makes implicit or explicit claims that the units of analysis from which the evidence is derived are appropriate to the task in hand.

## REVISION GUIDE

Representative sampling is discussed briefly in Unit 5, Section 1.2, and at length in Unit 8, see particularly Section 2.

Typicality, as opposed to representation, is discussed briefly in Unit 5, Section 3.1, and Unit 7, Section 2.

The different theoretical positions of empirical generalizations (to ultimately finite populations) and theoretical inferences (to potentially infinite populations) are discussed in Unit 7, particularly in Section 2.

---

We may also ask whether the cases are appropriate in the sense of being appropriate to the kind of evidence which is being collected. In Unit 9, for example, we looked in depth at surveys which collect information over the life-course as opposed to cross-sectional surveys which ask about present state and past state from the same people at the same time. It was argued that the former present much more credible evidence about changes over time than the latter, because of all the problems of memory and 'reconstruction' involved in questioning people about their past lives. This may be taken as a particular case of the more general question about whether the units of analysis are appropriate. At the simplest level of the question, we would clearly not be inclined to place much faith in research into student attitudes if the units of analysis were students who had only just arrived at the institution under investigation; they have had no time to form attitudes as students. Similarly we would not place much faith in research on patients' perceptions of nurses' attitudes if carried out on newly received patients, because they have not had time to assess these attitudes. A more complicated example, exhibiting what we called the ecological fallacy, arises in the comparison of Census wards on the dimensions of health status and material deprivation, which we have discussed in several units; if a correlation is observed, we still cannot assert that the people with poor health are those who are materially deprived because what we have measured are characteristics of wards, not characteristics of people.

When using quantitative 'secondary sources' this problem may often present itself as one of whether the appropriate population has been identified. When analysing crime statistics, for example, we are tempted to use them to draw conclusions about the types and incidence of crime. This is not correct, however, unless we can make a special argument that they are appropriate for the particular case which is being made. In general, crime statistics measure the number of incidents recorded by the police (on their own initiative or as a result of incidents being reported to them) and the number of people apprehended, charged and convicted; this is not the same thing as the number of crimes committed and the number of people committing them.

---

## REVISION GUIDE

The problems of sampling over time are discussed at length in Unit 9. See particularly Sections 1 and 2.

If you do not remember about the ecological fallacy, look back at the discussion in Unit 6, Section 3.

For a discussion of crime statistics, as a special case of correctly identifying an appropriate population using secondary sources, see Unit 5, Section 2.

---

What we are talking about here is part of the *logic* of a study — the way in which research is structured so that certain kinds of conclusions *can* logically be reached and supported. It embraces not only the kinds of subject studied, but also the data collected from or about them. Indeed, the two merge into each other. In a study of what babies like or dislike, we would not try to collect their verbal responses, because they do not *make* verbal responses; we would have to find some other way for them to make their likes and dislikes known (or rather, some form of measurement which we could *credibly argue* reflected what they liked or disliked). In the example in the last paragraph, we might be inclined to be sceptical about research on nurses' attitudes which collected information from any kind of patient, whether newly received or long established; it might seem more logical to collect the information from the nurses! On the other hand, a paper might argue that what could be collected from nurses would be the professional rhetoric of nursing, and that their individual attitudes to aspects of their job can better be judged by how they behave. In this case some kind of observation study would be the most obvious choice, but questioning patients about what *they* have observed might well be second best. In other words, one of the 'lower-level' arguments in a research paper — and it is an argument, not something that 'stands to reason' — concerns how the units of analysis and the data collected from or about them are positioned in the overall argument, from initial question to final conclusions, and whether they can logically bear that position.

## 2.2   THE SUITABILITY OF COMPARISONS

A crucial part of the argument of a research paper, in most cases, lies in the comparisons which it makes. This is most obviously displayed in experimental studies, where the structure of comparisons is crucial to the claims which the researcher will make: he or she must show that the experimental manipulation (and *only* that) led to the observed effect. Mostly this is done by comparing treated groups with untreated groups, or two or more differently treated groups, with all other aspects of the situation held constant; sometimes it involves comparing one state of a group of subjects with other states of the same group; the same logic holds. Many studies which are not experiments share the same logic, within the necessary imperfections of the situation, and their claims to credibility are tested in the same way. (The example which we used in Unit 6 was the 'Connecticut crackdown' (Campbell, 1969), the comparison of states which did or did not experience a change of policy with regard to speeding on the roads, but many other examples will spring to mind.) The same logic, indeed, may underlie studies which would not at all conceive of themselves as 'experiments' — for example, the Abbott and Sapsford (1987) study of mental handicap, which contrasted mothers of mentally handicapped children with other mothers in order to identify what was specific to the experiences of the former.

## REVISION GUIDE

The logic of experimentation is discussed in Unit 5, Section 1.3, and Unit 6, Sections 3 and 4.

The quasi-experimental analysis of non-experimental data is discussed in Unit 6, Section 3, and the use of a similar logic in non-quantitative studies is discussed in Unit 6, Section 5.

The Abbott and Sapsford paper, if you do not remember the details of it, will be found in Offprints Booklet 2.

Wherever an argument rests on a comparison (which is most of the time) a crucial question is *whether like is being compared with like*. In experiments this is guaranteed (or is supposed to be guaranteed!) by the structure of the research. In quasi-experimental comparisons more argument is needed to make the comparison credible: see, for example, the arguments which had to be brought forward in the 'Connecticut crackdown' study, and (perhaps more important) the respects in which its authors *could not* guarantee comparability between groups. This is a particular problem wherever data collected by others and/or for another purpose are being compared across time or between different countries. We saw in Unit 5, for example, that comparison of labour statistics across time are bedevilled by the different ways in which they have been collected (particularly in recent years). A paper I was commissioned to write some years ago (Banks and Sapsford, 1973), comparing the incidence of homicide between countries, degenerated into a comparison of the terminology used for homicide across Europe and North America; there was no way to compare the actual incidence. In other words, the different 'maps' used in different countries to categorize homicide into different kinds and, more important, to include some and exclude others from categories which might be seen as analogous to the British crime of 'murder', made it quite impossible to mount a sensible cross-national comparison using published statistics.

## REVISION GUIDE

The 'Connecticut crackdown' is discussed in Unit 6, Section 3.1.

The problems of comparison across time using published statistics are discussed in Unit 5, Section 2, through the example of labour statistics, and there is a wider discussion in Unit 13.

## 2.3   DATA COLLECTION AND MEASUREMENT

It is broadly true that researchers working within a quantitative framework speak of themselves as measuring variables, while qualitative researchers do not. However, both collect data and present them to the reader as part of the argument of research reports, and the problems they have in establishing that their conclusions follow from what they have collected show broad similarities. Note also that the division of researchers into 'quantitative' and 'qualitative' is too crude; these are data-collection styles, not characteristics of persons. The same researcher may espouse both styles, in different projects or even within the same project. In my own work on life-sentence prisoners (Sapsford, 1983), for example, the data collection involved long minimally-structured interviews with prisoners on how they experienced the sentence and what they did about it, *and* collection of descriptive and quantitative data from prison files (quarterly reports on the prisoner, and numbers of letters, visits, breaches of prison rules, etc.), *and* psychological personality and attitude measures of a greater or lesser degree of structure (inventories and questionnaires, but also 'projective' measures), *and* talking to key prison officers and governor-grade staff in general about lifers and their management, *and* a long period of 'hanging around the prison' seeing what was to be seen.

What is measured is not usually a direct representation of what the researcher wishes to discuss. An argument or *operationalization* is required to get from the researcher's concepts to the observable/measurable data which are collected and presented, and back from them to conclusions about the researcher's concepts. This holds as much in qualitative research as in quantitative, and as much for relatively simple concepts as for complicated ones.

With the kinds of complex concepts which are represented in research by *measurement scales* such as intelligence tests or personality inventories, the steps by which researchers (or their predecessors) go about validating the measuring instruments are well laid out, and the logic of them is apparent. Tests are validated by showing that the scales measure a single 'quantity' rather than several (*unidimensionality*), that they yield reasonably stable scores over time (*reliability*), that there is independent evidence that they do indeed measure what they purport to measure (*predictive validity* or *concurrent validity*) and that they 'behave' as the theory on which they are based says they should behave, discriminating where they should discriminate and failing to discriminate where they should fail to do so (*construct validation*).

Similar questions can be asked, however, of the least quantitative of researchers' constructs — those derived from 'unstructured' interviewing or observation: whether the classifications of opinion/memory or behaviour/interpretation which the researcher puts forward describe something which is stable rather than ephemeral, correctly identified and interpreted, and in agreement with previous theory in the area (or validly forcing a change on previous theory). Establishing validity convincingly is often more difficult in qualitative research because so much hangs on the researcher's individual observation and judgement, but this style also has its strategies for establishing the credibility of its conclusions. Often this may involve an appeal to other sources of data (*triangulation*), or an analysis of the social situation and how it was perceived by all participants (one aspect of *reflexivity*), or self-analysis to uncover and, perhaps, deal with prejudices and pre-conceptions (another aspect of *reflexivity*). Much can also be done to establish the credibility of conclusions by planned comparison of groups to test out the scope of theories (*theoretical sampling* and *analytic induction*) — a process which has much in common with construct validation.

We should note that these problems are not unique to qualitative research. Any research which is concerned with the past, even if its data are presented as numbers, suffers from problems of definition and has great difficulty establishing a basis of measurement on which like can be compared with like and conclusions drawn. For example, it is not a straightforward task to compare current incidence of marriage with practice in a world in which 'legal' marriage had to be solemnized by a priest, and where priests might visit some areas only infrequently or even be prohibited from carrying out such solemnization by papal interdict — i.e. some parts of England in the early middle ages. Indeed, as Unit 14 testified, elements of (often unacknowledged and generally undefended) judgement are exercised even in the coding of apparently 'factual' material from present-day surveys, and the coding may be as much influenced by previous theory as by the responses themselves.

## REVISION GUIDE

There is a general discussion of validity in Unit 3/4, Section 2.1. For the problems of operationalization, particularly as it applies to the construction of composite measures, see Unit 16, Section 2. Operationalization and concept formation in quantitative research are also discussed in Unit 11, Section 3.1, and the construction of composite measures is discussed in Unit 11, Section 3.3, and Unit 14, Sections 3.1 and 5.3. There is a useful summary of terms to do with validation in the glossary at the end of Section 2 of Unit 16. For the element of judgement involved in the coding of survey data, see Unit 14, particularly Sections 4, 5.2 and 5.3.

How the validity of conclusions from qualitative research is established is discussed in Unit 12, Section 5.2. See also specific discussions of triangulation in Unit 3/4, Section 3.2, and theoretical sampling and analytic induction in Unit 7, Section 3. (These are better conceived of as techniques for the generation of theory than as means of testing it — particularly theoretical sampling — but their use adds credibility to the argument that the conclusions are valid.)

# 3    RELEVANCE

When a research report's claims to truth have been evaluated, there are still many other sets of criteria on which it might properly be assessed. One of the most important of these, as we have said at several points during the course, is relevance. Although we are opposed to those who say that the *first* criterion of a good report is its usefulness, we accept that a research report is not much good unless it is good for something. However, 'relevance' is itself a relativistic criterion, and we may reasonably ask 'good for what?' and 'relevant for what?' Different audiences need different presentations and will undoubtedly take different kinds of conclusions out of the same piece of research, and the same presentation (in a journal, say) may be aimed at more than one audience. None the less the authors are expected to demonstrate its relevance to *some* audience, and their work may reasonably be judged on this criterion. In this section I will try to pull together some of what the course has had to say on the topic of relevance, under the headings of 'relevance for policy', 'relevance for practice' and 'research and theory'.

## 3.1   RELEVANCE FOR POLICY

The relationship of social research to social policy has never been a clear one. Cynics would argue that research has never helped to form policy, but only to confirm it — that government departments and politicians, for example, seek out and commission research that will appear to support them in the decisions they have already formed. At best, some would argue (e.g. Thomas, 1980) that research helps to *narrow the area of disagreement* in political and administrative debate, by outlining the size of the problem (or whatever) and describing its constituents. This would suggest that quantitative research would be more acceptable to policy-makers than qualitative studies, because of the supposed precision of numerical estimates and the air of 'scientificity' which they carry — as was argued, for example, in the Jayaratne article you read in association with Unit 16. This has indeed been the case until comparatively recently, but qualitative work is becoming increasingly acceptable and understood. Indeed, more and more studies now draw on elements of both approaches, trying to give *both* precision *and* insight, and more sponsors are now coming to expect this. We should note, however, that in highly politicized areas of policy the policy decision is unlikely to be deflected by mere numerical research. Much research has been done, for example, showing that the amount of money involved in fraudulent claims to unemployment and other benefits is tiny in comparison to the amount lost due to tax fraud on the part of companies and relatively wealthy individuals, but this has not changed the priorities which politicians have assigned to these two problems. (That it fails to do so perhaps suggests that the aims of the policies are not what politicians say they are — not increased efficiency in the spending of tax-payers' money, but the eradication of something seen as morally wrong in some absolute sense, and more wrong than company fraud.)

On the other hand, the case may be made that modern government could not run without research. Modern social policy is dependent on numerical information for its daily functioning: economic statistics, population statistics and projections, transport statistics, housing statistics, health and hospital statistics, statistics of the criminal justice system and the personal social services, education statistics, etc. (The collection of such statistics is often not classed as 'research', but research techniques are used and research decisions made.) There are also large areas of government action which have been very much influenced by social and educational research of a more academic kind. For example, in the field of education the work of psychological and educational theorists in the 1930s and 1940s had a great deal of influence on the establishment of the 'tripartite system' of streamed education (grammar, technical, secondary modern), and the work of educationalists and sociologists was equally influential in its replacement with the more egalitarian 'comprehensive system'. (Again, however, we can see from the example of educational policy how fragile the link between research and policy can be. Many of the changes being instituted in the early 1990s, at the time of writing, fly in the face of sound educational research, but this does not prevent them occurring.) Over and above its role as a servant of central government, local government and the like, social and educational research also serves policy-making by *informing* policy-makers and the 'general public'. Most of what we know is second hand, garnered from newspapers, television, books and what we are told and taught. Most of the information which we are told or taught is also second hand, derived from the same sources. It is social researchers who supply a great deal of this information and feed it into the system, and this has to count as an important policy-related outcome of research, because without it there would be no basis for judging what politicians and administrators do.

A part of this function, inevitably, is the critical appraisal and sometimes condemnation of what is going on. Social researchers are sometimes able to stand back from immediate debates in a way that those who are directly responsible for policy often cannot, and to take a critical approach, noting 'side effects' and unintended consequences, and assessing the amount of harm which policies do as well as the amount of good. This is not to say that they are neutral in the debates, of course, but that their livelihood does not currently depend on taking a line acceptable to government. (The extent to which they are able to take a line unacceptable to current government — the security of their tenure — varies from time to time and place to place, and it could be taken as an interesting indicator of a regime's fundamental liberality.) As has been pointed out since the 1960s, as well, the researcher and academic may be in a position to represent the views and needs of those who are otherwise unable to play an influential part in policy debates: the deprived, the disadvantaged, the inarticulate and in general 'the underdog'. In the field of health and community care, for example, a great deal of research effort has been expended on describing the lives and disadvantages of people with disabilities or mentally ill people or elderly people to 'the rest of the world', with the aim of overcoming prejudices and perhaps informing policy-makers, and many studies of prisons could be said to have the same aims. (That academic researchers do so from a privileged position, however, was pointed out in Unit 16.)

It remains to consider what is to be said about research which might be considered *too* relevant. In the first block of the course we spent some time considering what counts as research and what must be distrusted as propaganda. What do we say about researchers employed by trade unions, or employers, who manage to produce statistics which support the position taken by those who employ them? What do we say about researchers who are members of 'research institutes' known to have been founded to support a particular party political line? What do we say about research produced for or on behalf of influential pressure groups (ASH, Action on Smoking and Health, for example, or the tobacco trade) or about research produced for or on behalf of political parties themselves? As we indicated in Block 1, the answers to these questions are not as simple as they might appear. Political opinion polls, for example, are often commissioned by political parties or by newspapers with a declared alignment to a particular party, but this does not mean that the research they carry out is dishonest. Government researchers, and those employed in industry and by trade unions, are the same kind of people as are carrying out research in universities and independent institutes, thinking of themselves as part of the same research community and acknowledging themselves as bound by its conventions. There are pressures on them which are often not shared by academics, at the moment, but we should not wish to dismiss what they produce as mere propaganda. My own solution is that the reader of research needs to take account of the position adopted or supported by the researcher, and the source of the funds, but that this is only one element in our complex judgements of the credibility of research conclusions.

The same position must, of course, be adopted when reading the research of 'independent' researchers. It is a rare researcher who does not 'take a position' on the issues about which she or he is writing. The position may follow from the research, but it is more likely to precede it. In reading research we should make due allowance for the acknowledged 'position' of the researcher, and try to think of what might be said in opposition by those who take the opposite position; doing so is a standard 'tool of critique'. To the extent that it is possible, we should also take account of *un*acknowledged engagement of the researchers with their subject matter. The rare researcher may, perhaps, be genuinely neutral on a given topic, but for the most part it will be true that where preferences are not acknowledged they are unconscious rather than absent.

## REVISION GUIDE

The relevance of research for policy is discussed in Unit 3/4, Section 2.2, and Unit 10, Section 5. The discussion of the Jayaratne (1983) reading in Unit 16, Section 4, may also be seen as relevant. See also Unit 22, particularly Sections 2.3–2.5 and 4.

*reports to magit*
*reports of stewardship*
*'public interest' reports*

## 3.2   RELEVANCE FOR PRACTICE

A very large part of social and educational research is devoted to the work of social practitioners: social workers, health visitors, nurses, doctors, psychotherapists and counsellors, the police, prison staff, teachers and many more. (As you will see, the distinction between 'practice' and 'policy' is a very blurred one. We tend to identify work done at the boundaries of the two as 'policy' or 'practice' according to who does it, or who sponsors it, or which group most noticeably takes it up.) Traditionally, the most direct input of research into practice has been seen as happening in one of three ways.

First, research has been devoted to *exploring* the need for a given service. Most of the practitioners listed above make some use of descriptive statistics and descriptive surveys, directly in planning their own work or indirectly through the planning which their managers undertake. The need for income support, housing, school and hospital places and the like is determined in large part from descriptive statistics such as those collected annually by government and local government researchers, and these may also help the practitioner to plan for the *range* of likely clients (indicating the gender balance, racial mix and age structure of a catchment area, for example). More specific surveys are carried out where more detailed information is needed — for example, surveys of one-parent families to determine age, employment status, the condition of their housing, the health of their children and the state of their finances. From this kind of study a realistic idea can be formed of what services are needed, with what relative incidence, and (more important, perhaps) what problems are encountered which currently available services do not cover adequately. This is a kind of 'market research' for the public services, describing the relevant population and exploring needs. Some of this work is initiated by academics, but a lot of it is commissioned by agencies.

Secondly, research is used to *monitor* the performance of the public services and the practitioners who work in them. At a local level, surveys, and participant and interviewing studies examine the lives of clients and assess what impact the services which are provided are having on their problems. Others observe or ask questions about working practices, to describe them and enable good practice to be shared (and, sometimes, bad practice to be noticed). At a more global level, statistics are collected and used to match service provision to staffing levels, finances and the prevalence of need, and to compare the efficiency and effectiveness of different institutions. Again, some of this work is initiated by academics — in their role, sometimes, as critics of established practice and voices of those who would not otherwise be heard. Some is carried out in established research units set up for the purpose. Some is funded and commissioned by agencies keen to examine their own practice and to improve their own efficiency.

Thirdly, research has been used to *test* and evaluate *new* procedures and the impact of *new* policies. If money is being spent on a new facility or a new working practice it is becoming increasingly common to build evaluation procedures into it, or to commission a team to evaluate it, as evidence that the money is well spent and as a channel through which information can flow which will improve the new practice and keep it on course. Particularly in the areas of health, personal care and education, a great deal of published and unpublished research has been concerned to evaluate 'experimental' procedures. When the term 'evaluation study' comes up, people often tend to think first of experiments/controlled trials, or else more naturalistic studies which have some of the structure of experiments. More and more, however, studies of existing practice will have a qualitative element, or indeed will be entirely qualitative. Awareness is growing of the fact that detailed description of cases often has more impact on practitioners such as nurses, social workers or doctors than sets of figures, however logically convincing the latter may be. There is also growing awareness of the importance in evaluation of understanding the clients' point of view, the good and bad experiences they have, the part the treatment or intervention plays in the whole course of their daily lives, and the unexpected deleterious consequences which are possible from quite simple changes brought in with the best of intentions. Indeed, in some areas

*[handwritten margin notes:]*
- exploring the need for a (public) service
- monitoring the performance of (public) service & practitioners
- test & evaluate new procedures & impact of new policies

of research qualitative evaluation has been the dominant tradition for some while — the 'illuminative evaluation' of educational research, for example, or the case-study approach to co-operatives and small businesses.

There has been a growing fashion in the last decade or so for practitioners to argue that the best research, the most relevant for practice, will be that carried out by practitioners themselves. Only a practitioner, it is argued, can fully understand the nature of the particular practice in which she or he is engaged and of the particular clients for whom she or he caters, and practitioners know better than outside researchers what is practicable in the way of change. Thus we see an increasing advocacy of 'action research', by which is meant the monitoring of new procedures and policies by the same practitioners as are responsible for introducing them. There is also a growing advocacy, in health care and the social services, of the concept of 'the reflective practitioner' — the practitioner who automatically builds research and self-evaluation into his or her practice, so that research and practice become fully a part of each other. In the field of education the concept of 'the teacher as researcher' has some of the same force. It is argued that self-monitoring is more effective in many circumstances at changing and improving practice than monitoring by others, and that an element of self-monitoring helps to maintain the sensitivity and flexibility of practice.

Undoubtedly there is much to say for this position. 'Reflective practitioners' should, certainly, be more sensitive to the consequences of their practice and more open to change. (As practitioners who have carried out research into their own working practices and workplace will know, however, it can also be distracting and unsettling, making you self-conscious and sometimes making interaction with other workers more difficult and strained.) I am not inclined, however, to support the idea that *only* practitioners can carry out research on practice, nor necessarily to agree that they are always the best people to do so. Good research into practice often has the strength that it brings to the study of particular areas of work a wider context of knowledge and information than is generally available to any given practitioner. A social worker might be expert in social work, for example, but he or she is unlikely also to be as expert on racial divisions and discrimination, the needs and wishes of the elderly, or the developmental progress of children, as someone who is working full time on these specific aspects. Researchers are also able to 'move about the field' in a way that may often not be available to practitioners. Researchers in prisons, for example, can talk to prisoners, prison officers and prison governors on equal terms, while these three often cannot speak freely to each other. Thus, there is likely to be a continued role for research as distinct from practice, even if (as I hope) research attitudes become increasingly integrated into practice.

A final role for research in the service of practice, as in the service of policy, is the provision of information, insight and understanding. Researchers are able to bring parts of the 'field' into focus, bring theory to bear on them and sometimes 're-frame' them from an outside perspective, giving practitioners new ways of looking at what is most familiar to them, and sometimes, new understanding. Educational research, for example, has documented the inequality of teachers' interactions with boys and girls, and at the same time it has alerted teachers to why this might matter. Research into community care has shown how small the 'problem' is despite 'an ageing population' — how most people over 65 cope without help from statutory agencies, and how simple and specific the needs of the remainder often are. Research into the decisions made by parole boards has made visible to these boards the implicit policies on which they act. The list could be extended indefinitely.

## REVISION GUIDE

Gage's chapter in vol v.

You will find material relevant to this discussion in Unit 3/4, Section 2.2; Unit 5, Section 4, and Unit 10, Sections 4 and 5. See also Unit 22, particularly Sections 2.3 and 2.5.

## 3.3   RESEARCH AND THEORY

The other great popular stereotype of research, in the social field as well as the physical sciences, locates it as an activity undertaken by academics to test their theories. As we saw in Block 1, the relationship between theory and research is not quite as clear-cut as this. It has long been understood that no research study can prove a theory: if you get the results you expect on the basis of theory, they may have come about for the reasons which the theory gives, or for any number of other reasons. The accepted position in the philosophy of science for some time (most commonly associated with the work of Karl Popper) was that you cannot *prove* theories by research, but that you can *dis*prove them: while a positive result could come about for any number of reasons, a negative result where theory demanded a positive one points to disproof of the theory. Even this position is too simple, as we saw in Block 1, given the great body of theory out of which even the simplest research study emerges (theories which lead to the selection of operationalized measures and samples, for example). The truth of these 'auxiliary theories' or, in their totality, 'paradigms' would have to be beyond question before clear-cut and definitive disproof could emerge from a research study. We are also becoming increasingly aware that the credibility of research results rests on whole bodies of theory — 'world-models' or 'paradigms' — and not just on single testable theories. As we saw in Unit 16, for example, research on 'intelligence' depends on a 'world view' in which we can make sense of a fixed and measurable level of intellectual ability located within individuals; this view is dominant in our culture but other perspectives are possible. None the less it is true that theories about the social world have to be tested against the social world, that no way of understanding the world can ultimately be accepted which appears to be in outright contradiction to observed data, and that theories are judged against each other by the extent to which one perspective makes better or more inclusive sense of data than another.

A crucial role of research is in the *development* of ideas. In the development of theory, research is necessary to test out ideas, to familiarize oneself with changes in the field and to sensitize oneself to what is going on and how people are experiencing it. Exposure to what people say and do and to their conditions of life is also an excellent corrective to 'academic' theorizing, which can sometimes lose sight of the world it is trying to understand and focus on just a part of it which happens to be convenient for the line of theory. Theory, your own research and the research of others are the three legs of the academic tripod, and for the development of a stable and comprehensive understanding of the social world all three are necessary. Theory develops from immersion in the field and sensitizing yourself to the experienced realities of the area in which you are working, as much as from thinking about an area and trying to come up with testable ideas. At the same time the 'critical mind' is in play, trying to identify and see behind the presuppositions of those in the field, of other researchers and even of oneself.

## REVISION GUIDE

You will find relevant discussions in Unit 1/2, Section 6; Unit 3/4, Sections 2 and 3.4, and Unit 10 (particularly Section 2). Some of the material in Unit 21 might also be relevant. See also Unit 22, Sections 2.1 and 2.2.

# 4   PRECONCEPTION

The nature of a research study and its possible results are much determined by the preconceptions of the researcher (and/or the sponsoring or commissioning body). Part of the activity of the 'critical mind', whether in planning research or in assessing and interpreting research reports, lies in trying to be aware of likely preconceptions. How the research is framed from the start, for example, will determine the range that the results could possibly cover. A study of facilities available for youth in a local area will be different from a study of the problems of young people's behaviour in a given area, for example, even though the same lives and the same behaviours might be the target. Similarly a study of how to control or overcome examination anxiety would take different measures and attempt different solutions from a study of how to reduce the anxiety-provoking elements of the examination situation, though the same phenomenon is the target. The intention of the researchers, what they want *done* about the eventual results, can very easily become implicit in the way the 'problem' is formulated from the very beginning of the research. Similarly, early decisions about the 'natural' methods to use and the relationship between researchers and informants will also make a great deal of difference to the nature of the data collected and the conclusions reached. As Ruth Finnegan argues in Unit 10,

> ... the earlier choices which underlie research design, and the actual way that the design is manifested in the research process, are more than just technical questions (though they may have a technical side). They relate intimately to the underlying assumptions of the researcher. These underlying choices, furthermore, are likely to affect not only the overall plan, but also how empirical evidence is represented and co-ordinated, or the sources approached. The latter are not asocial 'data' just waiting there to be collected by some mechanical and neutral process, but are constructed according to the original selection of research topic and aims of the researcher.

> (Unit 10, Section 3.2)

There are traditions within disciplines and 'lines of research' about the appropriate kinds of method to use, which may amount to preconception. The study of human memory and cognition, for example, has been dominated since its inception by laboratory experiments. A great change in methodological paradigm took place in the 1970s and 1980s with the growth of usable computing resources and the possibility which the discipline seized on of developing and testing on computers competing models of how the human mind functioned. Back in the 1950s, however, a far greater methodological imagination was shown by Luria when he used essentially qualitative methods (interviewing and analysis of diaries) to explore the functioning of memory through intensive case studies of a mnemonist on the one hand and a brain-damaged man with short-term memory deficits on the other (Luria, 1968, 1972).

In other words, the traditional methods are not necessarily wrong or inappropriate, but often new insights proceed from finding new ways of coming at traditional problems; bringing some kind of 'triangulation' to bear within research traditions. Bringing innovative methods to bear on familiar problems often brings new and useful information or perspectives to light. In the counselling field, for example, a traditional way of exploring the relationship of past experiences to current problems had always been the long interview process, until George Kelly devised a pencil-and-paper 'test' (the Role Repertory Grid; see, e.g., Kelly, 1955) to cover some of the same ground; this has since been developed into a powerful research tool in a wide range of subject areas. In the field of personality measurement, the imaginative use of an interpersonal game to test the validity of the Machiavellianism Scale (Christie and Geiss, 1970), supposedly measuring a trait of tending to use others to achieve one's own ends, supplied valuable data not otherwise obtainable. When studying the behaviour and decision-making of professionals, a researcher can interview them and see what they *say* about their professional practice, or can study files or observe behaviour to see what they *do*, but both methods have substantial drawbacks — not least that the researcher has no control over the kinds of problem that will 'come up' and may be excluded from some on the grounds of sensitivity or professional ethics. The use of 'vignettes' as in the Dingwall and Fox (1986) paper which you read in Block 2, i.e.

brief descriptions of cases constructed by the researchers to be amenable to comparative analysis, gives a different perspective which has drawbacks of its own but overcomes some of the major drawbacks of the more traditional methods. Even more innovative, perhaps, is the recent research on legal decisions which presented solicitors (with their knowledge and consent) with faked 'real-life' cases presented by a real person and thereby came close to the conditions of a real legal consultation (Wasoff and Dobash, 1992).

Cultural preconceptions are also to be taken into account in planning or assessing research. We saw in Unit 16 the way that the sociological theory of class and class mobility, and associated research, tended until quite recently to take for granted a whole range of propositions about gender which owe more to ideology than to fact: that women have little stable connection with the world of work but are connected to it only through the social position of husbands or fathers; that a woman's position is in the home; and so on. Here the results of the preconception can be overcome to some extent once identified. Other ways in which ideology may become embedded in research are less easily overcome; all you can do is to identify them and bear them in mind. Research on work and working conditions, for example, could be seen by some as serving to reinforce the structures of a capitalist society; to make work more pleasant and more profitable while failing to change the structure of the ownership of capital sustains and supports the capitalist system. The same holds for much research commissioned by management; it may aim, and succeed, in making the lives of the managed more tolerable, but at the same time it strengthens the position of the management. A more subtle example of the acceptance by research of current forms of organization was discussed in Unit 16 — research into schooling and educational opportunity. To the extent that schooling methods are made more efficient and more palatable and accessible to children of a working-class background, access to power is spread down the social hierarchy and we move closer to a meritocracy. On the other hand, attracting the brightest of the working class into schooling means moving them out of the working class into middle-class jobs. Furthermore, the acceptance of schooling (as currently constructed) as a goal, could be seen as reinforcing one of our culture's dominant 'discourses' — the view of the social world as made up of individuals in competition, responsible for their failures and rewarded for their successes by social advancement.

Finally, in Unit 16 we raised one other area of preconception: the way in which we conceive of the research process itself. By tradition — and 'it stands to reason' — we conceive of research as being directed by researchers. It is researchers (and/or their sponsors) who decide to do it, plan it, carry it out, own the data and deliver the report. However, some feminists and also humanistic psychologists have questioned whether this structure really does 'stand to reason'. They suggest that it incorporates a power structure with the researcher in control and the researched as objects of manipulation or scrutiny; further, however much the researched or others like them stand to benefit from the research, one goal is the advancement of the researchers in terms of academic or research careers. It has been suggested that research should be based on informed consent and take the form of a collaboration to solve the problems of the researched, with the researcher's interests being subordinate to those of the researched. We pointed out problems with this view in Unit 16, but none the less it has something to commend it.

## REVISION GUIDE

See Unit 5, Unit 10 (particularly Section 3.2) and Unit 16, Sections 3 and 4. Some of Unit 21 might also be relevant.

# 5   ETHICS

A first principle of research ethics — to be found in all the various codes of conduct imposed by professional and academic organizations — is that the subjects of the research should not be harmed by it. You might think this fairly obvious, but some quite startling breaches of it have been committed in the course of research. In 1969, for example, a United States medical doctor called Godzeiher established a study to test the side effects of birth control pills which involved a 'control group' receiving only a placebo (a sugar pill) without their knowledge; seven unwanted pregnancies ensued. In the 1930s another US study sponsored by the public health service appears to have studied the course of syphilis by withholding treatment from 100 black sufferers, who were then examined and observed at intervals. Among projects which involved closer and more personalized interaction with the 'subjects' we might cite Milgram's work on conformity to authority, which involved subjects being put in the position of apparently administering near-lethal shocks to students in a learning task, and Zimbardo's 'simulated prison' experiment, where he divided a group of students up into 'prisoners' and 'guards' and set up a mock prison in a university basement (Haney *et al.*, 1973). Milgram's experiment, as he reports himself, left subjects anxious and shocked, and Zimbardo's had to be called off ahead of time because of the distress among some of the 'prisoners' and the uncontrolled behaviour of some of the 'guards'. I might also remind you of Seligman's 'learned helplessness' experiments on dogs which were described in Unit 6: somehow it seems no more acceptable to administer painful electric shocks to living creatures when they are dogs rather than people — less so if anything.

The counter-argument which might be put forward (and has been by Zimbardo, 1973) would be that the importance of the conclusions outweighed the pain caused by the research. Seligman would argue that exploring learned helplessness was important to clarify the theory of how we learn about our competence in the world, and as a clue to the aetiology and cure of human depression. Both Milgram and Zimbardo have justified their work by arguing that it was important to demonstrate in clear-cut and graphic terms the influence of situation on human behaviour. At a time when the atrocities of German and Japanese prison camps were being 'explained away' in terms of the national character of the Germans and Japanese, and the behaviour of prison guards and some police was attributed to their character and/or rough working-class upbringing, Milgram and Zimbardo demonstrated in their different ways that ordinary, middle-class people will oppress inferiors, beat them up and even apply torture on the instruction of an authoritative other or in response to their perception of the situation and its demands. Whether inflicting pain or distress is ever justified by the importance of the results, or how much pain is justified by how important a topic, is a question for each person to decide individually. It is an *open* question, however; even people vehemently opposed to murder might condone some particular act of assassination (e.g. of Hitler), and there comes a point in many people's thinking where one strong principle has to give way to another aspect of the public good.

Whatever your stance on these extreme studies, you ought to note that precisely the same ethical problems are faced, though in less dramatic form, by all experiments and many other research studies. We would generally agree that in 'ordinary' research the subject/informant/respondent should be protected from harm. It is for this reason, among others, that we generally promise informants confidentiality or anonymity in surveys or 'unstructured' interviewing projects: interviewing is intrusive, but having your personal details splashed in identifiable form across a research report is even more intrusive. (As I am using the terms, *confidentiality* is a promise that you will not be identified or presented in identifiable form, while *anonymity* is a promise that even the researcher will not be able to tell which responses came from which respondent.) It is generally argued that people should not be 'used' for research without their informed consent. Indeed, this principle goes a long way beyond research. It is normal for public documentary broadcasting to obtain the permission of people who have been filmed before the film is used (and this was done for the video sequences you looked at earlier in the course).

The concept of 'informed consent', however, is no easy answer to a set of moral dilemmas, because it is no simple and clear-cut thing itself. Very often in 'applied' research into social practice the researcher is a practitioner within the area of social practice and stands in a position of power or influence over the researched, or is identified with others who do so. The social worker, nurse, prison officer, or teacher, researching her or his own clients, patients, prisoners, or pupils, may have a direct power over the future of the people whom she or he wants as research informants. Even if not, there is an existing authority or dependency relationship such that the informants may feel bound to co-operate, however fairly and neutrally the request is put. It is also not clear whose informed consent is required, in many cases. In research into the treatment or handling of elderly people, do we need the consent of the elderly people themselves, or of their relatives, or of the district nurses and home helps who provide the immediate care, or of their general practitioners, or of the nursing and social services organizers, or of the management of the departments in which the practitioners work? All of these are 'interested parties' in the research, and many of them are or could be useful informants.

There is also the question of how far the consent can ever be 'informed'. To what extent, lacking the researcher's knowledge, can the other parties to the research ever understand fully what it is to which they are committing themselves and what use will be made of it? (You may remember the discussion in Unit 16 of the extent to which it is possible to share knowledge in collaborative research; this is another aspect of the same problem.) As researchers we are trusted on the whole by 'people out there' to behave honourably towards them, and they trust to some extent that the purpose of our research is important enough to justify the intrusion into their lives.

A related problem concerns those in whose lives we do *not* intervene. In a well-known educational experiment (Rosenthal and Jacobson, 1968), for example, the researchers picked children from a range of school classes at random and convinced the teachers that these had been identified as people likely to show a spurt of intellectual growth in the near future. Sure enough, some of these children did so, and the experiment is used as an example of the self-fulfilling prophecy in education. It may be seen as fundamentally ethical (except for the deception of the teachers) because no one was directly harmed by the intervention; children were either advantaged or left alone. If you were one of the 'control' children who were *not* randomly identified for development, however, and you read about the study afterwards, might you not feel that you too could have shown a spurt in school progress if the researchers had picked you for the experimental sample? The ethics of withholding a treatment which is expected to have a beneficial effect is a problem much discussed in practice research, particularly in education and medicine.

We should also note that even in qualitative approaches such as participant observation, often thought of as ethically 'cleaner' than experimental or survey research because there is no direct manipulation or interrogation of 'subjects', ethical problems remain. The most difficult of these concerns the relationships which are formed with participants and the use which is made of them. We tend to characterize participant observation and relatively unstructured interviewing as styles which give the participants a chance to express their own views and treat them as people in their own right. In practice, however, the conduct even of ethnographic research can be quite Machiavellian. In Jack Douglas' book *Investigative Social Research* (1976) — which you will find refreshingly cynical or surprisingly realistic, depending on your expectations — the chapter on tactics of investigative research has as sub-sections 'Infiltrating the setting', 'Building friendly trust and opening them up', 'Setting them up' and 'Adversary and discombobulating tactics'. In the first three of these he points out how ethnographers and social anthropologists slip into the setting like spies, building relationships for the purpose of using them to extract information.

> ... the right use of friendly and trusting relations is not only a necessity of research, but also a powerful one ... the extensive cultivation of friendly and trusting relations with people in all kinds of settings has been vital ... In building affection and trust it does not matter whether the researcher is honest or merely doing presentational work ... But he must be convincing.

> (Douglas, 1976, pp.134–7)

Douglas goes on to talk about normal aspects of intimate relationships — being prepared to reveal 'guilty facts' about yourself, for example — as deliberate tools of the social researcher, used to provoke similar disclosures. The role which the qualitative researcher presents in interactions is also under his or her control and 'imposed on' the participants — whether it be 'the acceptable incompetent' or 'the novice' or 'the ordinary citizen' or 'just a student', or whatever — and is selected to obtain maximum information at minimum discomfort.

In the 'setting up' section he talks about how ethnographers manipulate settings to their own advantage. This manipulation may be something as slight as interviewing people on their home ground so as to make the task less threatening, but Douglas also describes research into massage parlours in which he went to interview a journalist accompanied by two masseuses, and how the tone of the interview changed when he revealed their occupation. The section on adversarial tactics points out that not every qualitative project involves building friendly and trusting relationships; occasionally, particularly when dealing with the powerful, the tactic of outright but well informed attack may be more productive. All of this may seem distasteful, and some would say that researchers ought not to 'lie and cheat' in this manner, but others might equally validly point out that much research would be impossible if tactics such as these were *not* adopted.

Less discussed are wider ethical questions to do with the selection of problems and of samples. By studying the progress and problems of girls at school, for example, do we disadvantage boys? By looking at ways to make community care more effective for those who are receiving it, may we be doing the relatives or the professionals who administer it a disservice? Studying youth's behaviour in public, do we distract attention from their economic circumstances or the institutionalized behaviour of police and the criminal justice system? People may be harmed if their interests are not reflected in research, perhaps sometimes as surely as if they were physically or psychologically damaged. It was argued at one time, for example, that the tendency for sociological research to concentrate on the behaviour of working-class people was just one more facet of social control. Middle-class people learned from the research, and 'the system' became more effective in its control of the working class, but working-class interests were not served. (We should remember the contradiction pointed out above, however; if you wish to avoid research which will support the current forms of industrial organization, you will also have to avoid research which could make working conditions better for workers.)

I have raised a number of questions in this section and, I hope, failed to answer most of them. This is because of the position I take on the nature of ethical dilemmas. I am inclined towards a relativist position: that there are a large number of ethical imperatives, sometimes in conflict with each other, and that knowing that there can be ethical arguments against a course of action does not absolve the individual from considering the consequences of taking or refraining from the action. Others may take a more absolutist stand — that some things are in themselves wrong and should never be done, whatever the consequences. I would argue (but others would disagree) that there is no simple ethical code against which we can measure this research study or that; rather, there are a series of questions, some or all of which may need to be asked, and the answers weighed against the value of the study and the resources available to carry it out. They will include:

1   To what extent does the study involve deception, the use of the subjects/ respondents/informants/participants as objects for the researchers' purposes, or the betrayal of trust, confidence or intimacy?

2   To what extent does it involve harm or the possibility of harm — ranging from physical damage or psychological distress to the possibility of people *feeling* aggrieved or betrayed?

3   Who are the 'interested parties in the research', do they all get a chance to put their point of view, and has any group been overlooked?

4   Whose interests are served by the research?

Against the answers to these questions we would weigh the value of the research, the constraints which time and resources placed on the researchers, and the extent to which producing a study which was more acceptable in these respects would have weakened it as a vehicle for the discovery of truth.

There remains the question of what we do, as *readers*, about reports of studies which we consider grossly unethical or distasteful. I tend, myself, to use the results but to draw attention to the respects in which the study seems to me unacceptable in its methods. (I would hope to do this also when *writing* reports of my own research; many a study which seemed acceptable at the planning stage reveals itself as flawed with hindsight.) Others would refuse to have anything to do with such studies, arguing that to use an unethical study is to condone and encourage further such studies. Both positions are tenable; you will want to make up your own mind on this question, as on all the others throughout the course. You should also remember that you may not necessarily know that apparently-ethical projects have actually been carried out in ways of which you might not approve. Douglas (1976) points out that we all tell lies to each other in our ordinary lives, particularly lies of omission (concealing information which we consider discreditable to ourselves) and that this also happens in research accounts. Indeed, there is always the possibility that the 'information' with which we are being presented is partly or wholly fictional. We hope that the falsification of results and the concealment of methodological mistakes happens infrequently — the credibility of research is based on trust — but we can never be certain of any given piece of work. The furore in psychology when some of Cyril Burt's later work on the inheritance of intellectual ability was suspected of being based on made-up figures did not arise because such falsification was unthinkable. On the contrary, the force behind it stems from the fact that it is all too thinkable; we have all been tempted to 'improve' research accounts, at one time or another, and most of us have probably succumbed to the temptation, at least in minor form.

## REVISION GUIDE

Some of this material is discussed, in different ways, in Units 10, 12 and 16.

# REFERENCES

Abbott, P. and Sapsford, R. (1987) 'Leaving it to Mum', in *Community Care for Mentally Handicapped Children*, Chap. 2, Milton Keynes, Open University Press (reproduced in Offprints Booklet 2).

Abbott, P., Bernie, J., Payne, G. and Sapsford, R. (1992) 'Health and material deprivation in Plymouth', in Abbott, P. and Sapsford, R. (eds) *Research into Practice: a Reader for Nurses and the Caring Professions*, Buckingham, Open University Press.

Banks, C. and Sapsford, R. (1973) 'Some problems in the comparison of homicide figures', *Rassegna di Criminologia*, vol. 6, pp.9–34.

Campbell, D.T. (1969) 'Reforms as experiments', *American Psychologist*, vol. 24, pp.409–29.

Christie, R. and Geiss, F.L. (1970) *Studies in Machiavellianism*, London, Academic Press.

Dingwall, R. and Fox, S. (1986) 'Health visitors' and social workers' perceptions of child care problems', in While, A. (ed.) *Research in Preventive Community Nursing Care: Fifteen Studies in Health Visiting*, Chap. 12, Chichester, Wiley (reproduced in Offprints Booklet 2).

Douglas, J.D. (1976) *Investigative Social Research: Individual and Team Field Research*, Beverly Hills, Sage.

Hammersley, M. (ed.) (1993) *Social Research: Philosophy, Politics and Practice*, London, Sage (DEH313 Reader).

Haney, C., Banks, C. and Zimbardo, P.G. (1973) 'Interpersonal dynamics in a simulated prison', *International Journal of Criminology and Penology*, vol. 1, pp.69–97.

Jayaratne, T. (1983) 'The value of quantitative methodology for feminist research', in Hammersley, M. (ed.) (1993) (DEH313 Reader).

Kelly, G. (1955) *The Psychology of Personal Constructs*, New York, Norton.

Luria, A. (1968) *The Mind of a Mnemonist*, New York, Basic Books.

Luria, A. (1972) *The Man with a Shattered World*, New York, Basic Books.

Milgram, S. (1974) *Obedience to Authority: an Experimental View*, London, Tavistock.

Rosenthal, R. and Jacobson, L. (1968) *Pygmalion in the Classroom*, New York, Holt, Rinehart & Winston.

Sapsford, R.J. (1983) *Life-sentence Prisoners: Reaction, Response and Change*, Milton Keynes, Open University Press.

Thomas, R. (1980) 'Do statistics influence policy?', in D291 *Statistical Sources*, The Open University, Milton Keynes.

Wasoff, F. and Dobash, R.E. (1992) 'Simulated clients in "natural" settings: constructing a client to study professional policy', *Sociology*, vol. 26, pp.333–49.

Zimbardo, P.G. (1973) 'On the ethics of intervention in human psychological research', *Cognition*, vol. 2, pp.243–56.